Most Useful GERMAN Words

Joseph W. Moser, Ph.D.

DOVER PUBLICATIONS, INC.
Mineola, New York

Copyright

Copyright © 2012 by Joseph W. Moser
All rights reserved.

Bibliographical Note

2,001 Most Useful German Words is a new work, first published by
Dover Publications, Inc., in 2012.

Library of Congress Cataloging-in-Publication Data

Moser, Joseph W.
    2,001 most useful German words / Joseph W. Moser.
        p. cm. — (Dover language guides)
    Text in English and German.
    ISBN-13: 978-0-486-47626-1
    ISBN-10: 0-486-47626-X
    1. German language—Conversation and phrase books—English. 2. German
language—Grammar. 3. German language—Spoken German. I. Title. II. Title: Two
thousand one most useful German words.
PF3121.M59 2012
438.2'421—dc23

                                                                        2011050693

Manufactured in the United States by Courier Corporation
47626X03   2014
www.doverpublications.com

Contents

Introduction

This book contains over 2,000 useful German words intended to help beginners and intermediate speakers of German acquaint themselves with the most common and frequently used German vocabulary. Travelers to German-speaking Europe will also find this book useful, as it introduces many words they will encounter while in Austria, Germany, Switzerland, and other German-speaking regions. The reader can either go through the book alphabetically or skim here and there and enjoy picking up new German words and phrases. Unlike English, German nouns are divided into three genders: masculine, feminine, and neuter. Nouns in this book are followed by the abbreviations m., f., and n. to designate the gender. The plural ending for each noun follows in parenthesis, unless the stem-vowel changes in the plural form, in which case the reader will find the entire plural noun form in parenthesis. If the noun only exists in a plural form, the abbreviation pl. will follow the word. No reference to a plural form signifies that the singular and plural forms are identical; note that the article changes to "die" for all plural words. All German nouns are capitalized no matter where they are placed within a sentence. German word order allows for emphasized items in a sentence to be placed first. Only the verb has a required word order position as the second element in any sentence, therefore the reader will find that the word order in many of the German sentences differs from English, which requires the subject-verb word order in most sentences.

The first section of the book provides German words along with the English translation as well a German sentence using each word followed by the English translation of the sentence. The second part of the book lists common words by categories and includes a brief primer on German grammar. English and German are related Germanic languages, thus many of the high-frequency English words of Anglo-Saxon origin are similar to their German equivalents. The second part of the book also shows examples of cognates and words that are almost identical. When English speakers learn German, they should keep in mind that identifying similarities between the two languages will accelerate language acquisition. German and English grammars are also related, however, German retained many complex features that no longer exist in English, such as noun gender and case declentions.

Many of the example sentences are simple in order to allow the reader to quickly understand the context. Please note that many of the words have additional meanings, and thus the emphasis of this book is on the most common usages of a word. Of course, several of the words listed may also have other meanings in different contexts.

German is the most widely spoken language in the European Union and, with around 100 million speakers, is the native language of more Europeans than English, French, Italian, or Spanish. Given the economic strength of Germany, Austria, and Switzerland, many important companies across the world are operated by native German speakers, adding to the international significance of the language. The standard version of German is High German, or *Hochdeutsch*, which is the only accepted written form of modern German. Spoken German, however, differs regionally from the standard written form. There are many regional dialects, and it can be a lot of fun to pick up one of these dialects after spending an extended period of time in a particular region. Of course, High German is understood everywhere in German-speaking Europe, and in some areas of Western Germany, dialects have even been in decline. Regardless, dialects still remain strong in Austria, Switzerland, Luxembourg, Liechtenstein, and among German minorities living in other European countries such as Alsace and Lorraine in France as well as South Tyrol in Italy.

German Pronunciation Guide

German words are spelled more phonetically and systematically than English words, thus it is fairly easy to read and pronounce German words correctly.

Vowels

Vowels in German have the following sounds:

a	*ah*
e	*ay*
i	*ee*
o	*oh*
u	*oo*

Consonants

Many German consonants are similar to those in English except for:

g	always hard, as in the English word *go*
j	sounds like an English *y*
l	brief and not as drawn out as in English
r	rolled, similar to *r* in Spanish; in Northern Germany it comes from the back of the tongue/throat
s	sounds like an English *z*
v	sounds like an English *f* when at the start of a word
w	sounds like an English *v*
z	pronounced like *ts* in English

Diphthongs

au	*ow*
ch	non-existent in English, a guttural sound where the air passes over the tongue
ck	pronounced like a strong *k*
ei	*i*
eu	*oi*
ie	a long *ee*

Special German letters

ß	also knows as Eszett in German, sounds like a strong *s* in English
ä	similar to a German *e* or an English *eh*
ö	non-existent in English, sounds closest to *ur* with rounded lips
ü	non-existent in English, sounds closest to *ee-ew* with rounded lips

Alphabetical Section

A

ab   *down, off, starting from*
Ab heute kostet das Benzin wieder mehr.
Starting today, the price of gasoline is going up again.

Abend(-e) m.   *evening*
Am Abend geht Markus mit Freunden ins Kino.
In the evening, Markus goes to the movies with friends.

Abendessen n.   *dinner*
Zum Abendessen fahren wir heute ins Gasthaus.
Today we are going to a restaurant for dinner.

Abenteuer n.   *adventure*
Unsere Reise um die ganze Welt war für uns ein großes
Abenteuer.
Our trip around the world was a big adventure for us.

aber   *but*
Vielen Dank für das Angebot, aber das kann ich mir
nicht leisten.
Thanks for the offer, but I can't afford it.

Abfahrt(-en) f.   *ground vehicle departure*
Die Abfahrt des Intercity-Zuges nach Linz verspätet sich um
20 Minuten.
*The departure of the intercity train to Linz will be delayed by
20 minutes.*

Abflug(Abflüge) m.   *airplane departure*
Alle Abflüge innerhalb Europas gehen vom Terminal C am
Wiener Flughafen ab.
*All departures from the Vienna Airport to destinations within
Europe leave from Terminal C.*

abholen   *to pick up*
Die Mutter holt die Kinder von der Schule ab.
The mother is picking up her children from school.

Abitur n.   *high school final exam in Germany*
Wenn man das Abitur erfolgreich besteht, darf man in
Deutschland studieren.
*If you succesfully pass the high school final exam, you may study in
Germany.*

abkühlen   *to cool off*
An einem heißen Sommertag kann man sich mit einem Eis
abkühlen.
You can cool off with an ice cream on a hot summer day.

abmessen   *to measure*
Ich kenne meine Schuhgröße nicht, also muss ich meinen Fuß
abmessen.
I don't know my shoe size, so I will need to measure my foot.

abnehmen   *to lose weight*
Peter ist sehr glücklich, denn er hat mit seiner Diät 25 Kilo
abgenommen.
Peter is very happy because he lost 25 kilos on his diet.

abschalten   *to turn off*
Hier ist es sehr hell, also werde ich das Licht abschalten.
It is very bright in here, so I will turn off the light.

Abschied(-e) m.   *farewell, goodbye*
Der Abschied tut oft weh.
Goodbye often hurts.

achtung   *attention, beware*
Achtung auf Gleis 2! Zug fährt ein.
Attention on track 2! A train is arriving.

adoptieren   *to adopt*
Die Wicherts von nebenan adoptieren ein Kind.
The Wicherts from next door are adopting a child.

Adoption(-en) f.   *adoption*
Jede Adoption eines Kindes muss von den Behörden bewilligt
werden.
Every adoption of a child must be approved by the authorities.

ahnen   *to forsee*
Er hat geahnt, dass das nicht gut gehen kann.
He forsaw that this could not go well.

Ahnung(-en) f.   *idea*
Werner hatte keine Ahnung, dass die Steuern fällig waren.
Werner had no idea that taxes were due.

aktuell   *current*
Im Radio habe ich die aktuellen Nachrichten gehört.
I heard the current news on the radio.

Album(Alben) n.   *album*
Von unserer Reise in die Türkei habe ich ein Fotoalbum angefertigt.
I made a photo album of our trip to Turkey.

alle   *everyone*
Alle waren bei der Geburtstagsfeier.
Everyone was at the birthday party.

Allerlei pl.   *all kinds of*
In diesem Kaufhaus findest du allerlei Geschenkideen.
You will find all kinds of gift ideas in this department store.

Almanach(-e) m.   *almanac*
In einem Almanach kann man nützliche Informationen finden.
You can find useful information in an almanac.

Alpen   *Alps*
Die Alpen erstrecken sich von Frankreich bis nach Österreich.
The Alps stretch from France to Austria.

Alptraum(-träume) m.   *nightmare*
In der Nacht habe ich schlecht geschlafen, weil ich einen Alptraum gehabt habe.
I slept poorly last night because I had a nightmare.

also   *so, thus*
Es regnet heute, also müssen wir zu Hause bleiben.
It is raining today, so we need to stay home.

alt   *old*
Mein Auto ist so alt, dass ich ein Neues kaufen muss.
My car is so old that I need to buy a new one.

Altstadt(-städte) f.   *old town*
In der Altstadt von Nürnberg gibt es viele Sehenswürdigkeiten.
There are many sights to see in Nuremberg's old town.

Alufolie(-n) f.   *aluminum foil*
Sie wickelt das Fleisch in Alufolie.
She wraps the meat in aluminum foil.

Amerika   *America (usually in reference to North America or the United States)*
Amerika ist ein Kontinent in der westlichen Hemisphäre.
North America is a continent in the Western Hemisphere.

Amerikaner m. **Amerikanerin(-nen)** f.   *American person*
Frau Hess ist Amerikanerin aus New York.
Ms. Hess is an American from New York.

amerikanisch   *American*
Den Deutschen gefallen viele der amerikanischen Schnellimbissketten.
The Germans enjoy many of the American fast food chains.

Amt(Ämter) n.   *government office*
Auf dem Amt bekommen Sie Aukunft in behördlichen Angelegenheiten.
At the government office you can obtain information on offical matters.

an   *to, on*
Susanne schickt eine Mail an ihre Freundin in Wien.
Susanne sends an e-mail to her friend in Vienna.

anbieten   *to offer*
Heute bieten wir zwei Bücher zum Preis von einem an.
Today we are offering two books for the price of one.

anfangen   *to begin, to start*
Wir fangen heute mit der Arbeit an.
We are starting the work today.

angeben   *to show off*
Uwe gibt mit seinem großen Auto an.
Uwe is showing off with his big car.

Angelegenheit(-en) f.   *matter*
Das ist eine heikle Angelegenheit, über die man nicht mit allen sprechen darf.
This is a delicate matter that one is not allowed to speak of with others.

angenehm   *pleasant*
Er hat mit seinem Nachbarn ein angenehmes Gespräch geführt.
He had a pleasant conversation with his neighbor.

angestellt   *employed*
Ramona ist bei einer großen Bank in Zürich angestellt.
Ramona is employed with a large bank in Zurich.

Angst m.   *fear*
Wenn es dunkel ist, haben manche Menschen Angst.
Some people have a fear of the dark.

anhalten   *to hold on*
In der U-Bahn ist es ganz wichtig, dass man sich anhält, wenn der Zug fährt.
It is very important that you hold on tight when the subway train is moving.

Anker m.   *anchor*
Das Schiff legt den Anker an.
The anchor was thrown out of the ship.

ankommen   *to arrive*
Wir kommen am Sonntag um 15 Uhr in Basel an.
We will arrive in Basel at 3 pm on Sunday.

Ankunft(Ankünfte) f.   *arrival*
Die Ankunft des Fluges aus Prag ist für 18 Uhr vorgesehen.
The arrival of the flight from Prague is expected at 6 p.m.

Anlage(-n) f.   *plant*
Die Schulgruppe besucht die Anlage der Firma.
The school group visits the company's plant.

Anlass(-lässe) m.   *occasion, reason*
Der Anlass für die Ausstellung ist der 80. Geburtstag des Künstlers.
The reason for the exhibition is the artist's eightieth birthday.

annehmen   *to accept*
Wir nehmen die Bedingungen des Vertrags an.
We accept the conditions of the contract.

anrufen   *to call*
Sie können mich unter dieser Nummer anrufen.
You can call me at this number.

Ansicht(-en) f.   *opinion*
Meiner Ansicht nach ist die neue Initiative eine gute Idee.
In my opinion, the new initiative is a good idea.

Ansprache(-n) f.   *speech*
Er hat bei der Eröffnung der Ausstellung eine Ansprache
gehalten.
He gave a speech at the opening of the exhibition.

anstrengend   *exhausting*
Diese Arbeit ist sehr anstrengend.
This work is very exhausting.

Antrag(Anträge) m.   *application*
Frau Brenner geht auf das Passamt und stellt einen Antrag für
einen neuen Reisepass.
*Ms. Brenner goes to the passport office and files an application for a
new passport.*

Antwort(-en) f.   *answer*
Ich brauche eine Antwort auf meine Frage.
I need an answer to my question.

antworten   *to answer*
Die Frau Professor antwortet auf die Fragen der Studenten.
The professor answers the students' questions.

anzeigen   *to report, to charge*
Herr Müller zeigt seinen Nachbarn bei der Polizei an.
Mr. Müller reports his neighbor to the police.

anziehen   *to put on*
In der Früh ziehe ich mir eine Jacke an, bevor ich zur Arbeit gehe.
In the morning I put on a jacket before I go to work.

Arbeit(-en) f.   *work*
Herrn Vogel macht die Arbeit Spaß.
Mr. Vogel enjoys his work.

arbeiten   *to work*
Die meisten Deutschen arbeiten 40 Stunden pro Woche.
Most Germans work 40 hours per week.

Arbeitgeber m. **Arbeitgeberin(-nen)** f.   *employer*
Der Arbeitgeber zahlt die Sozialversicherung seiner
Arbeitnehmer.
The employer pays for his employees' benefits.

Arbeitnehmer m. **Arbeitnehmerin(-nen)** f. *employee*
Die Arbeitnehmer sind in der Gewerkschaft vertreten.
The employees are represented by a union.

arbeitslos *unemployed*
Bilge hat ihre Arbeit verloren und ist jetzt arbeitslos.
Bilge lost her job and is now unemployed.

Archiv(-e) n. *archive*
In einem Archiv werden alte Bücher und Dokumente gelagert.
Old books and documents are stored in an archive.

ärgern *to annoy*
Michael ärgert seine Kollegen.
Michael annoys his colleagues.

arm *poor*
Jakob ist ein armer Kerl, denn er hat sich das Bein gebrochen.
Jakob is a poor guy because he broke his leg.

Armut f. *poverty*
Die Armut ist ein großes soziales Problem in vielen Ländern der
  Welt.
Poverty is a significant social problem in many countries of the world.

Ass(-e) n. *ace*
Er hat vier Asse in der Hand.
He has four aces in his hand.

atmen *to breathe*
Wenn man sich erkältet, fällt es manchmal schwer zu atmen.
If you catch a cold, it can often be difficult to breathe.

auf *on*
Marika wohnt schon seit Jahren auf der spanischen Insel
  Mallorca.
Marika has been living on the Spanish island of Mallorca for years.

Aufenthalt(-halte) m. *stay*
Ich wünsche euch einen schönen Aufenthalt in Salzburg.
I wish you all a pleasant stay in Salzburg.

Aufenthaltstitel m. *residence permit*
Manche Ausländer brauchen einen Aufenthaltstitel, um in
  Deutschland zu wohnen.
Some foreigners need a residence permit to live in Germany.

aufführen   *to perform*
Im Wiener Burgtheater werden immer wieder interessante
   Theaterstücke aufgeführt.
They always perform interesting plays at Vienna's Burgtheater.

Aufführung(-en) f.   *performance*
Die Aufführung von Wagners Ring-Zyklus an der Staatsoper war
   ausgezeichnet.
*The performance of Wagner's Ring Cycle at the State Opera was
   excellent.*

Aufgabe(-n) f.   *task*
Es ist meine Aufgabe die Wohnung zu putzen.
It is my task to clean the apartment.

aufgeben   *to mail*
Er hat gestern den Brief aufgegeben.
He mailed the letter yesterday.

aufheben   *to pick up*
Er hebt den Zettel vom Boden auf.
He picks up the note from the floor.

aufhören   *to cease, to stop*
Die Nachbarn hören mit dem Lärm auf.
The neighbors stop making noise.

aufmachen   *to open*
Ich mache ihr die Tür auf.
I am opening the door for her.

Aufmerksamkeit(-en) f.   *attention*
Der Bürgermeister dankt den Anwesenden für ihre
   Aufmerksamkeit.
The mayor thanks those present for their attention.

aufpassen   *to watch out*
Pass auf, wenn du über die Straße gehst.
Watch out when you cross the street.

aufregend   *exciting*
Gestern haben wir einen aufregenden Film gesehen.
Yesterday we saw an exciting movie.

aufsperren   *to unlock*
Der Herr sperrt die Tür auf.
The gentleman unlocks the door.

aufstehen   *to stand up, to get up (from bed)*
Herr Kreisky steht von einem Nachtmittagsschläfchen auf.
Mr. Kreisky gets up from an afternoon nap.

aufwachen   *to wake up*
Jeden Morgen wache ich auf, wenn die Sonne aufgeht.
Every morning I wake up when the sun rises.

aufwachsen   *to grow up*
Die Kinder wachsen schnell auf.
The children grow up quickly.

aufwärmen   *to warm up*
Im Winter kann man sich in vielen deutschen Städten mit einem
   Glas Glühwein aufwärmen.
*During the winter, you can warm up in many German cities with a
   glass of mulled wine.*

Aufzug(-züge) m.   *elevator*
Mit dem Aufzug fährt man bequem in den 8. Stock.
You can easily reach the 8th floor with the elevator.

Augenblick(-e) m.   *moment*
Kannst du für einen Augenblick zu mir kommen?
Could you come here for a moment?

Auktion(-en) f.   *auction*
Bei der Auktion haben wir diese schöne Vase erstanden.
We purchased this pretty vase at the auction.

aus   *out (of)*
Gisela nimmt die Milch aus dem Kühlschrank.
Gisela takes the milk out of the refrigerator.

Ausdruck(Ausdrücke) m.   *expression*
In einer Fremdsprache will man immer den treffenden Ausdruck
   finden.
One always wants to find the exact expression in a foreign language.

Ausfahrt(-en) f.   *highway exit*
Bei der Ausfahrt 51 biegen Sie bitte links ab.
Please turn left at highway exit 51.

Ausflug(Ausflüge) m.   *excursion*
Am Wochenende machen wir einen Ausflug in die Berge.
This weekend we will go on an excursion to the mountains.

ausführlich   *in detail*
> Die Nachrichten haben ausführlich über den Unfall berichtet.
> *The news reported in detail on the accident.*

Ausgang(Ausgänge) m.   *exit*
> Der Ausgang aus dem Museum befindet sich links von der
> Eingangstür.
> *The museum exit is located to the left of the entry door.*

ausgehen   *to go out*
> Jeden Freitagabend gehen wir aus.
> *We go out every Friday evening.*

ausgezeichnet   *excellent*
> In diesem Gasthaus haben wir ein ausgezeichnetes Wiener
> Schnitzel gegessen.
> *We ate an excellent wiener schnitzel at this inn.*

Auskunft(Auskünfte) f.   *information*
> Berthold bittet den Schaffner um Auskunft nach der Abfahrtszeit
> des Zuges.
> *Berthold asks the conductor for information about the train's departure
> time.*

Auslage(-n) f.   *store window*
> Viele Geschäfte in deutschen Einkaufsstraßen haben schöne
> Auslagen.
> *Many stores on German shopping streets have nice window
> displays.*

Ausland n.   *abroad*
> Sie wohnen im Ausland.
> *They live abroad.*

Ausländer m. **Ausländerin(-nen)** f.   *foreigner*
> Peter aus Chicago ist Ausländer ist Deutschland.
> *Peter from Chicago is a foreigner in Germany*

ausmalen   *to paint (a wall)*
> Die Frankes malen ihr neues Esszimmer aus.
> *The Frankes are painting the walls of their new dining room.*

Ausrede(-n) f.   *excuse*
> Das ist natürlich eine gute Ausrede.
> *Of course that is a good excuse.*

aussehen   *to appear*
Die Situation in der Krisenregion sieht nicht gut aus.
The situation in the crisis region does not appear good.

außen   *outside*
Außen hui und innen pfui!
Pretty on the outside and ugly on the inside.

außer   *except for*
Alle außer dir haben mir ein Geburtstagsgeschenk gekauft.
Everyone except for you bought me a birthday present.

aussteigen   *to exit a vehicle*
Das ist die Endstation, bitte alle aussteigen!
This is the final stop, everyone please get off!

Ausstellung(-en) f.   *exhibition*
Im Museum gibt es eine neue Ausstellung über die Geschichte
   des Landes.
There is a new exhibition on the country's history at the museum.

Australien n.   *Australia*
Australien ist ein Land auf der südlich des Äquators.
Australia is a country south of the equator.

Australier m. **Australierin(-nen)** f.   *Australian person*
Paul ist Australier und kommt aus Melbourne.
Paul is an Australian and comes from Melbourne.

australisch   *Australian*
Australische Fernsehserien kann man auch im deutschen
   Fernsehen sehen.
You can also see Australian TV series on German TV.

Austropop m.   *Austrian pop music*
Der Austropop ist in Österreich und Deutschland sehr beliebt.
Austrian pop music is very popular in Austria and Germany.

Ausverkauf(-käufe) m.   *sale*
Alle Hemden sind im Ausverkauf.
All shirts are on sale.

Auswahl f.   *selection*
Dieses Buch bietet eine Auswahl der bedeutendsten Gedichte des
   Dichters.
This book offers a selection of the poet's most important poems.

Ausweis(-e) m.   *identification*
Um diese Karte zu kaufen, müssen Sie Ihren Ausweis zeigen.
In order to buy this ticket, you have to show your I.D.

Auto(-s) n.   *car*
Mit dem Auto gelange ich schneller zur Arbeit als zu Fuß.
I get to work faster by car than by foot.

Autobahn(-en) f.   *highway*
Die deutschen Autobahnen sind in der ganzen Welt bekannt, weil
man sehr schnell fahren kann.
*German highways are famous throughout the world since you can drive
very fast on them.*

Autobus(-se) m.   *bus*
Der Autobus halt um die Ecke in der Friedrichstraße.
The bus stops around the corner on Friedrich Street.

B

Baby(-s) n.   *baby*
Das Baby schläft tagsüber und schreit in der Nacht.
The baby sleeps during the day and screams at night.

Babynahrung(-en) f.   *baby food*
Babynahrung findet man in Deutschland in jeder Drogerie.
You can find baby food at every drugstore in Germany.

Bach(Bäche) m.   *small stream*
Im Bach schwimmt eine schnelle Forelle.
A fast trout swims in the small stream.

Backblech(-e) n.   *baking sheet*
Frau Gstettner backt Plätzchen mit dem Backblech.
Ms. Gstettner bakes cookies on a baking sheet.

backen
Der Bächer backt jeden Morgen frische Semmeln.
The baker bakes fresh rolls every morning.

Backform(-en) f.   *baking pan*
Sie backt einen Kuchen in der Backform.
She is baking a cake in the baking pan.

baden   *to bath, to swim*
Im Sommer baden viele Wiener in der Donau, um sich
abzukühlen.
During the summer, many Viennese swim in the Danube to cool off.

Badewanne(-n) f.   *bathtub*
Im Badezimmer findest du eine große Badewanne.
In the bathroom you will find a large bathtub.

Badezimmer n.   *bathroom*
Das Badezimmer befindet sich im 2. Stock.
The bathroom is located on the second floor.

Bahnhof(-höfe) m.   *train station*
Zum Bahnhof gelangen Sie in Zürich mit der Straßenbahn.
You can reach the train station in Zurich by streetcar.

Bahnsteig(-e) m.   *railway platform*
Achtung Bahnsteig 12! Ein Zug fährt durch.
Attention platform 12! A train is coming through.

bald   *soon*
Wir sehen uns bald wieder.
We will see each other again soon.

Ball(Bälle) m.   *ball*
Im Februar kann man in Wien auf verschiedenen Bällen tanzen.
You can dance at several balls in Vienna in February.

Band(Bände) m.   *volume*
Dieses Lexikon hat 15 Bände.
This encyclopedia has 15 volumes.

Band(Bänder) n.   *ribbon*
Ich binde das Paket mit einem Band zu.
I tie the package with a ribbon.

Band(-s) f.   *musical band*
Die Band ist sehr beliebt bei Jugendlichen.
The band is very popular with teenagers.

Bank(Bänke) f.   *bench*
Im Park setze ich mich gerne auf eine Bank.
I like to sit on a bench in the park.

Bankomat(-en) m.   *automatic teller machine (ATM)*
Am Bankomat kann man Bargeld beheben.
You can withdraw cash from the ATM.

Bargeld n.   *cash*
In Deutschland wird Bargeld Kreditkarten in Geschäften
  vorgezogen.
In Germany, stores prefer cash over credit cards.

Basketball spielen   *to play basketball*
In der Slowakei spielen viele junge Männer Basketball.
Many young men in Slovakia play basketball.

Bauernhof(-höfe) m.   *farm*
Manche Familien in Österreich machen im Sommer gern Urlaub auf dem Bauernhof.
Some families in Austria like to spend their summer vacation on a farm.

Baum(Bäume) m.   *tree*
Im Herbst verlieren die Bäume ihre Blätter.
In fall the trees lose their leaves.

Baumwolle f.   *cotton*
Das Hemd ist aus Baumwolle.
The shirt is made of cotton.

beantragen   *to apply*
Er beantragt seine Rente.
He applies for his retirement pay.

bearbeiten   *to work on*
Frau Schneider bearbeitet Ihren Antrag.
Ms. Schneider is working on your application.

Becher m.   *cup*
Er trinkt Wein aus dem schönen Becher.
He drinks wine from the pretty cup.

bedanken   *to thank*
Herr Groer bedankt sich für die Blumen, die er zum Geburtstag bekommen hat.
Mr. Groer thanks the person who got him flowers for his birthday.

bedeuten   *to mean*
Was bedeutet dieses große Schild auf der Straße?
What does this big sign on the road mean?

bedeutend   *significant*
Die Arbeit des Schriftstellers ist ein bedeutender Beitrag zur Literatur des Landes.
The writer's work is a significant contribution to the country's literature.

befinden   *to be located*
Sie befinden sich hier auf der Karte.
You are located here on the map.

befördern   *to promote*
Er ist in seiner Firma befördert worden.
He was promoted in his company.

Befund(-e) m.   *findings*
Der ärztliche Befund zeigt, dass der Patient gesund ist.
The doctor's findings show that the patient is healthy.

begeistern   *to fascinate*
Wir sind vom neuem Buch des Autors begeistert.
We are fascinated by the author's new book.

begraben   *to bury*
Mozart liegt in Wien begraben.
Mozart is buried in Vienna.

Begräbnis(-se) n.   *funeral*
Das Begräbnis findet morgen auf dem Friedhof statt.
The funeral will take place tomorrow at the cemetery.

behalten   *to keep*
Das Rückgeld können Sie behalten.
You can keep the change.

Behälter m.   *container*
In dem Behälter neben dem Kühlschrank findest du den Zucker.
You'll find the sugar in the container next to the fridge.

behandeln   *to treat*
Der Arzt behandelt einen Patienten.
The physician is treating a patient.

Behandlung(-en) f.   *treatment*
Durch die Behandlung ist der Patient wieder gesund geworden.
Due to the treatment, the patient became healthy again.

behaupten   *to claim*
Manfred behauptet, dass diese Fussballmannschaft gewonnen hat.
Manfred claims that this soccer team won.

Behörde(-n) f.   *authority*
Das muss ich der Behörde melden.
I need to report this to the authority.

bei   *at, near*
Bei meiner Tante bekommen wir heute Abendessen.
We will have dinner at my aunt's today.

Beilage(-n) f.　　*side dish*
Als Beilage zu meinem Schnitzel möchte ich Pommes.
I'd like a side of fries with my schnitzel.

beinahe　　*almost*
Darauf habe ich beinahe vergessen.
I almost forgot about that.

Beispiel(-e) n.　　*example*
Das ist ein gutes Beispiel für einen schönen Aufsatz.
This is a good example of a nice essay.

beißen　　*to bite*
Achtung! Diese Hunde beißen.
Watch out! These dogs bite.

Beißkorb(-körbe) m.　　*muzzle*
Hunde dürfen nur mit einem Beißkorb und an der Leine ins
　　Geschäft.
*Dogs can only come into the store if they have a muzzle and are on a
　leash.*

Beitrag(-träge) m.　　*contribution*
Sein Beitrag zum Projekt ist sehr wichtig.
His contribution to the project is very important.

beitreten　　*to join*
Er tritt dem Sportverein bei.
He joins the sport club.

bekannt　　*well-known*
Die Lieder dieser Sängerin sind im ganzen Land bekannt.
*This singer's songs are well-known throughout the whole
　country.*

Bekannte(-n) m. and f.　　*acquaintance*
Frau Mayer ist eine Bekannte von mir.
Ms. Mayer is an acquaintance of mine.

Bekanntschaft(-en) f.　　*acquaintance*
Im Urlaub haben wir mehrere Bekanntschaften geschlossen.
We made several acquaintances during our vacation.

bekommen　　*to receive*
Zum Geburtstag bekommt er immer viele Geschenke.
He always gets lots of presents for his birthday.

belegen   *to take a university course*
Er belegt dieses Semester drei Vorlesungen in Germanistik.
He is taking three lecture classes in German Studies this semester.

beleidigen   *to insult*
Jakob hat Rudi beleidigt und jetzt sind sie nicht mehr Freunde.
Jakob insulted Rudi and now they no longer friends.

Beleidigung(-en) f.   *insult*
Persönliche Beleidigungen sind in Deutschland strafbar und
  können vor Gericht abgehandelt werden.
*Personal insults are punishable by law in Germany and can be dealt
  with in court.*

Belgien n.   *Belgium*
Im Königreich Belgien spricht man Französisch, Flämisch, aber
  auch Deutsch.
*In the Kingdom of Belgium they speak French, Flemish, and also
  German.*

beliebt   *popular*
Diese Musik ist beliebt bei jung und alt.
This music is popular with young and old people.

benehmen   *to behave*
Die Kinder haben sich gut benommen und keinen Lärm gemacht.
The children behaved well and didn't make a sound.

Benehmen n.   *behavior*
Dein schlechtes Benehmen hat mich sehr verärgert.
Your bad behavior made me very upset.

benötigen   *to need*
Ich benötige ein Visum, um in dieses Land zu fahren.
I need a visa to travel to this country.

beobachten   *to observe*
Die Mutter hat die Kinder vom Fenster aus beobachtet.
The mother observed the children from the window.

bequem   *comfortable*
Franz sitzt in einem bequemen Sessel.
Franz sits in a comfortable chair.

beraten   *to advise*
Der Professor berät die Studenten.
The professor advises his students.

bereit   *ready*
Ich bin bereit, die Prüfung zu schreiben.
I am ready to take the exam.

Berg(-e) m.   *mountain*
Der Großglockner ist der höchste Berg in Österreich.
The Grossglockner is the highest mountain in Austria.

Bericht(-e) m.   *report*
Er hat einen interessanten Bericht in der Zeitung geschrieben.
He wrote an interesting report in the newspaper.

berichten   *to report*
Frau Müller berichtet von ihrer Geschäftsreise nach Amerika.
Ms. Müller reports about her business trip to North America.

beruhigen   *to calm down*
Nach dem Unfall hat man versucht, sie zu beruhigen.
They tried to calm her down after the accident.

berühmt   *famous*
Der berühmte Schauspieler hat vor der Premiere seines neuen
     Filmes Autogramme gegeben.
The famous actor signed autographs before the premiere of his
     new film.

Bescheid(-e) m.   *notification*
Ich habe den Bescheid von der Behörde erhalten, dass ich Steuern
     nachzahlen muss.
I received notification from the authorities that I need to pay back taxes.

bescheiden   *modest*
Jens hat zu seinem Geburtstag nur bescheidene Wünsche.
Jens only has modest wishes for his birthday.

beschlagnahmen   *to confiscate*
Die Polizei hat das Auto des Verbrechers beschlagnahmt.
The police confiscated the criminal's car.

beschließen   *to decide on*
Die Regierung hat beschlossen, die Steuern zu senken.
The government decided to lower taxes.

beschreiben   *to describe*
Könnten Sie mir bitte den Weg zum Museum beschreiben?
Could you please describe the way to the museum?

Beschreibung(-en) f.   *description*
Der Beschreibung nach sollte das Haus vier Schlafzimmer.
*According to the description, the house is supposed to have four
    bedrooms.*

Beschwerde(-n) f.   *complaint*
In Antwort auf die Beschwerde sind die Angestellten in der
    Firma jetzt freundlicher zu den Kunden.
*In response to a complaint, the company's employees are now friendlier
    to the customers.*

beschweren   *to complain*
Herr Klein hat sich über den Lärm der Nachbarn bei der Polizei
    beschwert.
Mr. Klein complained to the police about the noise from his neighbors.

besichtigen   *to sightsee, to visit*
In Wien haben wir natürlich den Stephansdom besichtigt.
We visited St. Stephen's Cathedral in Vienna, of course.

Besichtigung(-en) f.   *visit*
Nach der Besichtigung des Schloss Schönbrunn haben wir im
    Kaffehaus eine heiße Schokolade getrunken.
*After a visit to the Schönbrunn Palace, we drank a hot chocolate at the
    café.*

besitzen   *to own*
Er besitzt dieses große Auto.
He owns this large car.

besonders   *especially*
Diese Blumen sind ganz besonders schön.
These flowers are especially pretty.

Besteck n.   *cutlery*
Das Besteck wird in der Spülmaschine gewaschen.
The cutlery is being washed in the dishwasher.

bestehen   *to consist*
Die Wagentür besteht aus Metall.
The car door consists of metal.

bestellen   *to order*
Er bestellt ein Schnitzel mit Kartoffelsalat.
He orders a schnitzel with potato salad.

bestrafen   *to punish*
Der Richter bestraft den Mann für zu schnelles Fahren.
The judge punishes the man for driving too fast.

besuchen   *to visit*
Peter besucht seine Familie in Innsbruck.
Peter is visiting his family in Innsbruck.

beten   *to pray*
Wir beten für die Opfer des Unfalls.
We pray for the victims of the accident.

betragen   *to amount to*
Die Kosten für Ihren Aufenthalt im Krankenhaus betragen
500 Euro.
The cost for your stay at the hospital amounts to 500 euros.

betreiben   *to run, to operate*
Die Familie betreibt ein Restaurant in Basel.
The family runs a restaurant in Basel.

betrügen   *to cheat*
Dieser Verkäufer hat mich betrogen, denn er hat mir zu wenig
Rückgeld erstattet.
This salesperson cheated me because he didn't give me enough change.

Bett(-en) n.   *bed*
Im Kinderzimmer stehen zwei kleine Betten.
In the children's room there are two small beds.

Bettwäsche f.   *bed linen*
Die Bettwäsche wird in der Waschmaschine gewaschen.
The bed linens are being washed in the washing machine.

beunruhigen   *to worry*
Die Nachrichten haben viele Menschen beunruhigt.
The news worried many people.

beurteilen   *to judge*
Es ist schwer zu beurteilen, was tatsächlich passiert ist.
It is difficult to judge what actually happened.

Bevölkerung(-en) f.   *populace, population*
Die Bevölkerung der Stadt hat einen neuen Bürgermeister
gewählt.
The city's populace elected a new mayor.

bevor *before*
Bevor wir nach Hause fahren, gehen wir noch einkaufen.
Before we go home, we will go shopping.

bewachen *to guard*
Der Hund bewacht sein Haus durch lautes Bellen.
The dog guards his houses by barking loudly.

bewölkt *cloudy*
Heute sieht man die Sonne nicht, weil es stark bewölkt ist.
You can't see the sun today because it is very cloudy.

bewundern *to admire*
Er bewundert die Gemälde im Museum.
He admires the paintings in the museum.

bezahlen *to pay*
Nach dem Essen im Restaurant muss man die Rechung bezahlen.
After eating in a restaurant, you have to pay the bill.

Bezirk(-e) m. *district*
Die Stadt Wien ist in 23 Bezirke eingeteilt.
The city of Vienna is divided into 23 districts.

bezweifeln *to doubt*
Ich bezweifle, dass der Flug pünktlich ankommen wird.
I doubt that the flight will arrive on time.

Bibliothek(-en) f. *library*
In der Bibliothek kann man Bücher ausleihen.
You can borrow books from the library.

Biergarten(-gärten) m. *beer garden (in Bavaria)*
In Bayern findet man im Sommer leicht einen Biergarten.
You can easily find a beer garden in Bavaria in summer.

Bild(-er) n. *picture, image*
Auf dem Bild sieht man alle Familienmitglieder.
You can see all the family members in the picture.

Bilderrahmen m. *picture frame*
Sie kauft sich einen Bilderrahmen für das Familienporträt.
She buys a picture frame for the family portrait.

billig *inexpensive, cheap*
Peter möchte eine billige Uhr kaufen.
Peter wants to buy a cheap watch.

Biologie f.   *biology*
Die Biologie ist eine Naturwissenschaft, die man an der
Universität studieren kann.
Biology is a natural science that you can study at university.

bisschen   *little*
Geben Sie mir bitte ein bisschen vom Schinken.
Please give me a little bit of the ham.

bitte   *please*
Können Sie mir bitte die Tür aufmachen?
Could you please open the door for me?

bitten   *to ask for*
Dürfte ich Sie um Auskunft bitten?
May I ask you for some information?

bitter   *bitter*
Diese Orange schmeckt mir nicht, weil sie so bitter ist.
This orange does not taste good to me because it is so bitter.

blasen   *to blow*
Wenn die Suppe zu heiß ist, muss man auf sie blasen, damit sie
sich abkühlt.
*If the soup is too hot, you have to blow on it so it will cool
down.*

Blatt(Blätter) n.   *leaf*
Im Herbst fallen die Blätter von den Bäumen.
In fall the leaves fall from the trees.

bleiben   *to stay*
Nach dem Unterricht bleiben wir in der Klasse und sprechen mit
dem Lehrer.
*After the lesson we stay in the classroom and speak with the
teacher.*

Bleistift(-e) m.   *pencil*
In der ersten Klasse dürfen die Schüler noch mit Bleistift
schreiben.
In first grade, students are still allowed to write with a pencil.

blind   *blind*
Die junge Frau ist blind und kann nicht sehen.
The young lady is blind and cannot see.

Blitz(-e) m.   *lightning, flash*
Der Blitz hat in das Dach des Hauses eingeschlagen und großen
  Schaden verursacht.
Lightning hit the roof of the house and caused a lot of damage.

Blume(-n) f.   *flower*
Im Stadtpark haben wir viele interessante Blumen gesehen.
We saw many interesting flowers in the city park.

Blumenstrauß(-sträuße) m.   *bouquet of flowers*
Jan hat seiner Frau zum Geburtstag einen Blumenstrauß
  geschenkt.
Jan gave his wife a bouquet of flowers for her birthday.

Blut n.   *blood*
Manchmal muss der Arzt bei der Untersuchung Blut
  abnehmen.
Sometimes a physician needs to draw blood during an examination.

Boden(Böden) m.   *floor, soil*
Die meisten Deutschen und Österreicher mögen es nicht, auf
  dem Boden zu sitzen.
Most Germans and Austrians don't like to sit on the floor.

Bodensee m.   *Lake Constance*
Der Bodensee liegt zwischen Österreich, Deutschland und der
  Schweiz.
Lake Constance lies between Austria, Germany, and Switzerland.

Bordkarte(-n) f.   *boarding card*
Zum Einstieg ins Flugzeug benötigen Sie eine Bordkarte.
In order to board the plane, you need a boarding card.

böse   *evil*
Die böse Hexe hat die Kinder in ihr Knusperhäuschen gelockt.
The evil witch lured the children into her gingerbread house.

Botschaft(-en) f.   *embassy*
Herr Schuster beantragt einen neuen Reisepass in der
  Botschaft.
Mr. Schuster applies for a new passport at the embassy.

brauchen   *to need*
Wir brauchen noch Zucker und Mehl, um den Kuchen zu
  backen.
We still need sugar and flour to bake the cake.

brav   *well-behaved*
   Die Kinder waren gestern so brav.
   The children were really well-behaved yesterday.

BRD(Bundesrepublik Deutschland) f.   *FRG (Federal Republic of Germany)*
   Die BRD wurde im Jahre 1949 gegründet.
   The FRG was founded in 1949.

brechen   *to break*
   Wir brechen gemeinsam das Brot.
   We break bread together.

Bremse(-n) f.   *brake*
   Die Bremsen müssen auf diesem Wagen gerichtet werden.
   The brakes on this car have to be fixed.

bremsen   *to brake*
   Uschi bremst schnell, um nicht über das auf der Autobahn stehende Wildschwein zu fahren.
   Uschi brakes quickly to avoid hitting the wild boar standing on the highway.

Brett(-er) n.   *board*
   Die Brotzeit wird üblicherweise auf einem Brett serviert.
   The snack is typically served on a board.

Brettspiel(-e) n.   *board game*
   Am Wochenende hat die Familie ein lustiges Brettspiel gespielt.
   Over the weekend, the family played a fun board game.

Brief(-e) m.   *letter*
   Dein Brief ist noch immer nicht angekommen.
   Your letter still hasn't arrived.

Briefkasten(-kästen) m.   *mailbox*
   Der Briefkasten wird ein Mal pro Tag geleert.
   The mailbox is emptied once per day.

Briefmarke(-n) f.   *postage stamp*
   Briefmarken kann man auf dem Postamt kaufen.
   You can buy stamps at the post office.

Brille(-n) f.   *eyeglasses*
   Ohne Brillen kann ich nicht sehen.
   I can't see without my glasses.

bringen   *to bring*
Bitte bring mir die Zeitung.
Please bring me the newspaper.

Brücke(-n) f.   *bridge*
Die Brücke führt über den Rhein von der Schweiz nach
   Deutschland.
The bridge extends over the Rhine from Switzerland to Germany.

brüllen   *to scream*
Die Fans brüllen beim Fußballspiel.
The fans scream during the soccer game.

brutal   *brutal*
Der brutale Verbrecher sitzt jetzt im Gefängnis.
The brutal criminal is now in prison.

Buch(Bücher) n.   *book*
Der Autor signiert sein Buch.
The author signs his book.

Bücherei(-en) f.   *public library*
Er holt sich ein Buch aus der Bücherei.
He is getting a book from the public library.

Bücherregal(-e) n.   *bookshelf*
Im Wohnzimmer stehen zwei Bücherregale.
There are two bookshelves in the living room.

Bucht(-en) f.   *bay*
Die Fischer sind in die Bucht zurückgekehrt.
The fishermen returned to the bay.

Bund(Bünde) m.   *federation*
Der Bund zahlt für die Schulen.
The federation pays for the schools.

Bundesheer n.   *Austrian Armed Forces*
Das Bundesheer ist das Militär in Österreich.
The Bundesheer is Austria's military.

Bundeskanzler m. **Bundeskanzlerin(-nen)** f.   *chancellor
   (in Austria and Germany)*
Der Bundeskanzler führt die Regierung in Österreich und
   Deutschland.
The chancellor leads the government in Austria and Germany.

Bundesland(-länder) n.   *state within Germany or Austria*
Rheinland-Pfalz ist ein Bundesland der Bundesrepublik
    Deutschland.
Rhineland-Pallatine is a state in the Federal Republic of Germany

Bundespräsident(-en) m. **Bundespräsidentin(-nen)** f.   *federal*
    president
Der Bundespräsident ist das Staatsoberhaupt in Österreich,
    Deutschland und der Schweiz.
The federal president is the head of state in Austria, Germany, and
    Switzerland.

Bundesrepublik(-en) f.   *federal republic*
Deutschland ist eine Bundesrepublik mit 16 Bundesländern.
Germany is a federal republic with 16 states.

Bundeswehr f.   *German military*
Die deutschen Soldaten dienen in der Bundeswehr.
German soldiers serve in the German military.

Burg(-en) f.   *castle*
Neuschwanstein ist eine weltberühmte Burg in Bayern.
Neuschwanstein is a world famous castle in Bavaria.

Bürger m. **Bürgerin(-nen)** f.   *citizen*
Die Bürger wählen am Sonntag.
The citizens vote on Sunday.

Bürgermeister m. **Bürgermeisterin(-nen)** f.   *mayor*
Der Bürgermeister eröffnet eine neue Schule.
The mayor opens a new school.

Büro(s) n.   *office*
Er arbeitet im Büro.
He is working in the office.

Bürste(-n) f.   *brush*
Er putzt sich die Schuhe mit einer Bürste.
He cleans his shoes with a brush.

bürsten   *to brush*
Die Kinder bürsten sich die Zähne.
The children are brushing their teeth.

Busch(Büsche) m.   *bush*
Eine Katze versteckt sich hinter dem Busch.
A cat is hiding behind the bush.

C

Celsius   *centigrade*
Heute hat es 25 Grad Celsius.
Today's temperature is 25 degrees centigrade.

Cent m.   *cent*
Jeder Euro hat 100 Cent.
Each euro contains 100 cents.

Chance(-n) f.   *chance*
Er verdient noch eine weitere Chance.
He deserves one more chance.

Chanukka n.   *Hanukkah*
Chanukka ist ein wichtiger Feiertag im Judentum.
Hanukkah is an important holiday in Judaism.

Chaos n.   *chaos*
Nach dem Erdbeben herrschte in der Stadt das Chaos.
The city was filled with chaos after the earthquake.

chaotisch   *chaotic*
Die Zustände am Flughafen waren chaotisch.
The conditions at the airport were chaotic.

Charakter m.   *character*
Er hat einen guten Charakter.
He has good character.

charakteristisch   *typical*
Das ist charakteristisch für seine Arbeit.
That is typical of his work.

charmant   *charming*
Oft hört man, dass die Wiener charmant sind.
It is often said that the Viennese are charming.

Charme m.   *charm*
Leider hat er seinen Charme verloren.
Unfortunately, he lost his charm.

Chef(-s) m.   *boss*
Der Chef hat dieser Frau gekündigt.
The boss fired the woman.

Chemie f.   *chemistry*
Anton hat Chemie an der Universität studiert.
Anton studied chemistry at the university.

Chor(Chöre) m.   *choir*
Die ganze Familie singt im Chor.
The entire family sings in the choir.

Christ(-en) m. **Christin(-nen)** f.   *Christian*
Er ist Christ.
He is a Christian.

Christentum n.   *Christianity*
Das Christentum ist eine der wichtigsten Religionen der Welt.
Christianity is one of the most important religions in the world.

Creme(-s) f.   *cream*
Frau Kanka verwendet jeden Tag diese Creme.
Ms. Kanka uses this cream every day.

D

da   *there*
Da sehe ich eine alte Kirche.
I see an old church over there.

dabei   *with it*
Die Batterien sind in der Packung der Fernbedienung dabei.
The batteries are included in the package with the remote control.

Dach(Dächer) n.   *roof*
Alle Häuser in Graz haben rote Dächer.
All houses in Graz have red roofs.

Dachboden(-böden) m.   *attic*
Auf dem Dachboden lagern alte Möbel.
Old furniture is being stored in the attic.

dafür   *for it*
Er ist dafür, dass die Steuern gesenkt werden.
He is for lowering taxes.

dagegen   *against it*
Ich bin dagegen, dass hier ein Einkaufszentrum errichtet
    wird.
I am against a mall being built here.

daheim   *at home*
Die Schneiders sind in Baden-Württemberg daheim.
The Schneiders are at home in Baden-Württemberg.

damals   *back then*
Damals gab es noch kein Internet.
Back then, there was no internet.

Dame(-n) f.   *lady*
Die Dame hat sich eine Handtasche gekauft.
The lady bought a purse.

Damm(Dämme) m.   *dam*
Das Wasser ist über den Damm gelaufen.
The water ran over the dam.

Dampf(Dämpfe) m.   *steam*
Aus dem Bad kommt viel Dampf.
A lot of steam is coming from the bathroom.

danach   *after that*
Erst gehen wir ins Theater und danach ins Restaurant.
First we are going to the theater and after that to the restaurant.

Dänemark n.   *Denmark*
Frau Andersen wohnt in Kopenhagen und kommt aus
   Dänemark.
Ms. Andersen lives in Copenhagen and comes from Denmark.

dänisch   *Danish*
Brigitte fährt im Sommer gern an die kühlen dänischen
   Strände.
Brigitte likes to travel to the cool Danish beaches in summer.

dankbar   *grateful*
Herr Müller ist seinem Nachbarn dankbar für die Hilfe im
   Garten.
Mr. Müller is grateful for his neighbor's help with the gardening.

danke   *thank you*
Danke für die Blumen!
Thank you for the flowers!

danken   *to thank*
Paul dankt seiner Familie für die vielen Geburtstagsgeschenke.
Paul thanks his family for the many birthday presents.

dann   *then*
Wenn wir nicht genug Zeit haben, dann machen wir das nicht.
If we don't have enough time, then we won't do that.

darstellen   *to depict*
Der Schauspieler hat Napoleon gut dargestellt.
The actor depicted Napoleon well.

dass   *that*
Ich glaube, dass es morgen regnen wird.
I think that it will rain tomorrow.

Date(-s) n.   *date*
Udo hat morgen ein Date mit seiner Freundin.
Udo has a date with his girlfriend tomorrow.

Datum(Daten) n.   *date*
Welches Datum haben wir heute?
What is today's date?

dauern   *to last*
Die Führung dauert etwa 2 Stunden.
The guided tour lasts about 2 hours.

DDR(Deutsche Demokratische Republik) f.   *GDR (German Democratic Republic)*
Die DDR existierte von 1949 bis 1990 im Osten Deutschlands.
The GDR existed in East Germany from 1949 to 1990.

Decke(-n) f.   *blanket*
Er deckt sich mit einer Decke zu.
He covers himself with a blanket.

dehnen   *stretch*
Die Lederhosen haben sich durch regelmäßiges Tragen gedehnt.
The lederhosen stretched after being worn regularly.

dementieren   *to deny*
Der Präsident dementiert seine Rolle im Skandal.
The president denies his role in the scandal.

Demokratie(-n) f.   *democracy*
Die Demokratie hat sich in Deutschland erst in der zweiten Hälfte des 20. Jahrhunderts etabliert.
Democracy was not established in Germany until the second half of the 20th century.

denken   *to think*
Wenn er reist, denkt er oft an seine Familie zu Hause.
When he travels, he often thinks of his family at home.

Denkmal(-mäler) n.   *monument, memorial*
Neben dem Brandenburger Tor in Berlin befindet sich das
   Denkmal für die ermordeten Juden in Europa.
*The Memorial to the Murdered Jews of Europe is located next to the
   Bradenburg Gate in Berlin.*

denn   *because*
Wir bleiben zu Hause, denn das Wetter ist nicht gut genug, um
   zu wandern.
*We are staying at home because the weather isn't good enough to go
   hiking.*

Deo(-s) n.   *deodorant*
Deos bekommt man in Deutschland in jeder Drogerie.
You can buy deodorant at every drugstore in Germany.

deshalb   *therefore*
Die U-Bahn war verspätet und deshalb kam er spät zur Arbeit.
The subway was delayed and he was therefore late for work.

deutsch   *German*
Sie isst gern deutschen Käse.
She likes to eat German cheese.

Deutschland n.   *Germany*
Deutschland befindet sich in Mitteleuropa.
Germany is located in Central Europe.

Deutsche(-n) m./f.   *German*
Frau Lange ist Deutsche und kommt aus Leipzig.
Ms. Lange is German and comes from Leipzig.

Diamant(-en) m.   *diamond*
Diamanten kann man beim Juwelier kaufen.
You can buy diamonds at the jewelers.

Diät(-en) f.   *diet*
Hans ist auf Diät und isst nur gesundes Essen.
Hans is on a diet and only eats healthy foods.

dick   *fat, large*
Diese Katze ist dick, weil sie zu viel isst.
This cat is fat because she eats too much.

dienen *to serve*
Der Soldat dient seiner Heimat.
The soldier serves his homeland.

Dienstleistung(-en) f. *services*
Unsere Firma bietet verschiedene Dienstleistungen an.
Our company offers various services.

Diktatur(-en) f. *dictatorship*
In einer Diktatur gibt es keine Demokratie.
There is no democracy in a dictatorship.

Dinosaurier m. *dinosaur*
Die Kinder sehen gern die Dinosaurier im Museum.
The children like to look at the dinosaurs in the museum.

Disko(-s) f. *dance club*
Jugendliche gehen am Wochenende gern in die Disko.
Teenagers like to go to the dance club on the weekend.

Diskussion(-en) f. *discussion*
Die Diskussion hat bis lang in die Nacht gedauert.
The discussion lasted late into the night.

diskutieren *to discuss*
Die Gruppe diskutiert das Buch.
The group is discussing the book.

Distanz(-en) f. *distance*
Bei einer Distanz von fast 800 km, braucht man mit dem Auto
7 Stunden von Zürich nach Wien.
*At a distance of almost 800 kilometers, it will take 7 hours by car to
drive from Zurich to Vienna.*

Dom(-e) m. *cathedral*
Der Stephansdom in Wien ist einer der imposantesten im
deutschsprachigen Europa.
*St. Stephan's Cathedral in Vienna is one of the most impressive in
German-speaking Europe.*

Donner m. *thunder*
Ich höre Donner und sehe Blitzschäge.
I hear thunder and see lightning.

doppelt *double*
Wir haben den doppelten Preis bezahlt.
We paid double the price.

Dorf(Dörfer) n.   *village*
Im Dorf wohnen etwa 523 Einwohner.
About 523 residents live in the village.

dort   *there*
Dort findest du viele Restaurants.
You'll find many restaurants there.

Dose(-n) f.   *can*
Er isst Bohnen aus der Dose.
He is eating beans from a can.

Drache(-n) m.   *dragon*
Der böse Drache wohnt in einer Höhle.
The evil dragon lives in a cave.

draußen   *outside*
Draußen hat es nur 4 Grad, was recht kalt ist.
It is only 4 degrees outside, which is really cold.

drehen   *to turn*
Er dreht den Schlüssel in der Tür.
He turns the key in the door.

drinnen   *inside*
Drinnen ist es schön warm.
It is nice and warm inside.

drohen   *to threaten*
Er droht uns mit der Polizei, wenn wir nicht sofort weggehen.
He is threatening to call the police if we don't leave immediately.

Druck(Drücke) m.   *pressure*
Der Druck ist unter Wasser höher.
The pressure is higher underwater.

drücken   *to push*
Drücken Sie bitte um die Tür zu öffnen.
Please push on the door to open it.

Duft(Düfte) m.   *scent*
Mir gefällt dieser Duft, weil er mich an Rosen erinnert.
I like this scent because it reminds me of roses.

duften   *to smell (pleasant)*
Dieses Parfüm duftet hervorragend.
This perfume smells wonderful.

dulden   *to tolerate*
Rauchen wird in diesem Haus nicht geduldet.
Smoking is not tolerated in this house.

dunkel   *dark*
Wenn es dunkel wird, muss man das Licht andrehen.
You have to turn on the light when it gets dark.

dünn   *thin*
Sie schneidet sich eine dünne Scheibe Brot.
She is cutting a thin slice of bread.

Dunst(Dünste) m.   *haze*
Wenn viele Leute im Zimmer rauchen, gibt es einen blauen Dunst
    in der Luft.
When a lot of people smoke in a room, there is a blue haze in the air.

durch   *through*
Wir fahren durch den Tunnel.
We are driving through the tunnel.

Durchschnitt(-e) m.   *average*
Im Durchschnitt verkehren auf dieser Straße 2.000 Autos pro Tag.
On average, 2,000 cars travel on this road every day.

durchschnittlich   *on average*
Durchschnittlich 35.000 Autos verkehren täglich auf der A1 in
    Salzburg.
On average, 35,000 cars travel daily on the A1 in Salzburg.

dürfen   *to be allowed to*
Die Kinder dürfen draußen spielen.
The children are allowed to play outside.

Dusche(-n) f.   *shower*
Der Installateur repariert die kaputte Dusche.
The plumber repairs the broken shower.

duschen   *to shower*
Jeden Morgen duscht sich Heino vor der Arbeit.
Every morning Heino takes a shower before work.

E

Ebbe(-n) f.   *low tide*
Es ist besser bei Ebbe am Strand zu spazieren.
It is better to go for a walk on the beach during low tide.

eben *just*
Ich habe eben mit der Lehrerin gesprochen.
I just spoke with the teacher.

Ecke(-n) f. *corner*
Die Katze schläft auf einer Decke in der Ecke.
The cat is sleeping on a blanket in the corner.

edel *noble*
Das ist ein ganz altes edles Geschäft.
This is a very old and noble store.

Effekt(-e) m. *effect*
Bertolt Brecht hat in seinem Theater den Verfremdungseffekt
eingeführt.
Bertolt Brecht introduced the alienation effect in his theater pieces.

egal *equal, the same*
Das ist mir egal.
It's all the same to me.

ehe *before*
Ehe wir abreisen können, müssen wir das Haus putzen.
Before we can leave, we have to clean the house.

Ehe(-n) f. *marriage*
Die Ehe wird jetzt aufgelöst.
The marriage is being dissolved.

ehemalig *former*
Dresden ist eine Stadt auf dem Gebiet der ehemaligen DDR.
Dresden is a city in former GDR territory.

Ehre(-n) f. *honor*
Ich habe die Ehre, unseren Gast vorzustellen.
I have the honor of introducing our guest.

ehrlich *honest*
Er hat die Liste ehrlich erstellt.
He compiled the list honestly.

Eidgenossenschaft(-en) f. *confederation (Switzerland)*
Die Schweiz ist eine Eidgenossenschaft mit 23 Kantonen.
Switzerland is a confederation of 23 cantons.

Eifersucht f. *jealousy*
Eifersucht ist keine Tugend.
Jealousy is not a virtue.

eifersüchtig   *jealous*
Er ist eifersüchtig ihren Erfolg.
He is jealous of her success.

eigentlich   *actually*
Eigentlich will ich dieses Jahr im Urlaub in die Türkei fahren.
I actually want to go to Turkey for vacation this year.

Eigentum n.   *property*
Diese Bücher sind sein Eigentum.
These books are his property.

Eimer m.   *bucket*
Der Eimer ist voll mit Wasser.
The bucket is filled with water.

Einbahnstraße(-n) f.   *one-way street*
In einer Einbahnstraße muss man in die richtige Richtung fahren.
On a one-way street, you have to drive in the correct direction.

Eindruck(-drücke) m.   *impression*
Ich habe den Eindruck, dass es dir gut geht.
I get the impression that you are doing well.

einfach   *simple*
Das ist eine einfache Geschichte.
This is a simple story.

Einfluss(-flüsse) m.   *influence*
Er hat keinen Einfluss auf den Prozess.
He has no influence on the process.

einführen   *introduce*
Der Betriebsleiter führt den neuen Kollegen in die Firma ein.
The supervisor introduces the new colleague to the company.

Einführung(-en) f.   *introduction*
Der Professor hat die Einführung zum Buch geschrieben.
The professor wrote the introduction to the book.

eingebildet   *arrogant*
Florian ist sehr eingebildet und nicht nett zu seinen Freunden.
Florian is very arrogant and not nice to his friends.

Einheit(-en) f.   *unit*
Wir lesen zwei Einheiten des Textbuches.
We are reading two units of the textbook.

einkaufen   *to shop*
Die Familie kauft im Supermarkt ein.
The family is shopping in the supermarket.

Einkäufer m. **Einkäuferin(-nen)** f.   *shopper*
Der Einkäufer nimmt an einer Umfrage teil.
The shopper participates in a survey.

Einkaufskorb(-körbe) m./f.   *shopping basket*
Sie legt die Einkäufe in den Einkaufskorb.
She puts the purchases in the shopping basket.

Einkommen n.   *income*
Das durchschnittliche Einkommen ist in der Schweiz höher als in
   Deutschland.
The average income in Switzerland is higher than in Germany.

einladen   *to invite*
Wir laden unsere Freunde zu einem Fest ein.
We are inviting our friends to a party.

Einladung(-en) f.   *invitation*
Ich habe eine Einladung zu einer Geburtstagsfeier erhalten.
I received an invitation to a birthday party.

einlangen   *arrive, receive*
Die neue Ware ist im Geschäft eingelangt.
The new goods arrived at the store.

Einleitung(-en) f.   *introduction (of a book)*
Der Autor hat eine gute Einleitung zu seinem Buch
   geschrieben.
The author wrote a good introduction to his book.

einsetzen   *to appoint*
Er wurde als Chef der Firma eingesetzt.
He was appointed head of the company.

einsteigen   *to board a vehicle*
Bitte alle einsteigen! Der Zug fährt ab.
All aboard! The train is departing.

Einwohner m.   *inhabitant*
Die Einwohner der Stadt haben gegen den Bau der Brücke
   gestimmt.
The city's inhabitants voted against the bridge's construction.

Eis n.   *ice, ice cream*
Ich will kein Eis in meinem Getränk.
I don't want any ice in my beverage.

Eisen n.   *iron*
Die Brücke ist aus Eisen.
The bridge is made of iron.

Eisenbahn(-en) f.   *railroad*
Die Eisenbahn hat keinen Bahnhof in dieser Stadt.
There is no railroad station in this city.

eisig   *icy*
Draußen ist es heute wirklich sehr eisig.
It is really icy outside today.

Eiswürfel m.   *ice cube*
Ich möchte keine Eiswürfel in meinem Getränk.
I don't want any ice in my drink.

eitel   *vain*
Sie ist sehr eitel und schaut sich ständig im Spiegel an.
She is very vain and constantly looks at herself in the mirror.

eklig   *gross*
Er hat den ekligen Käse aus dem Kühlschrank weggeworfen.
He threw away the gross cheese from the fridge.

Elfenbein n.   *ivory*
Diese kleine Figur ist aus Elfenbein.
This small figurine is made of ivory.

Email n.   *enamel*
Der Topf ist aus Email.
The pot is made of enamel.

Empfang(-fänge) m.   *reception*
Bei dem Empfang haben wir viele Freunde getroffen.
We met many friends at the reception.

empfangen   *to receive*
Ich habe dein Paket schon in der Post empfangen.
I already received your package in the mail.

empfehlen   *to recommend*
Ich werde den Kellner fragen, was er heute empfiehlt.
I will ask the waiter what he recommends today.

empfindlich   *sensitive*
Meine Zähne sind sehr empfindlich auf kalte Getränke.
My teeth are very sensitive to cold drinks.

emsig   *busy, diligent*
Sie haben emsig die Arbeit abgeschlossen.
They diligently completed the work.

Ende(-n) n.   *end*
Das Ende des Filmes hat mir sehr gut gefallen.
I really liked the end of the movie.

endlich   *finally*
Endlich sind wir nach dem achtstündigen Flug in Florida
   angekommen.
After an eight-hour flight, we finally arrived in Florida.

Engel m.   *angel*
Brigitte glaubt an Engel.
Brigitte believes in angels.

England n.   *England*
England ist ein Land im Westen der Europäischen Union.
England is a country in the western part of the European Union.

Engländer m. **Engländerin(-nen)** f.   *English person*
Herr McCartney ist Engländer aus Liverpool.
Mr. McCartney is an Englishman from Liverpool.

englisch   *English*
Er kauft gern englische Anzüge.
He likes to buy English suits.

enorm   *enormous*
Das ist ja ein enorm großes Haus.
This is really an enormously large house.

entbehren   *to live without*
Derzeit kann er leider kein Geld entbehren.
Unfortunately, he can't live without money at this point.

entdecken   *to discover*
Ein Wikinger hat Nordamerika entdeckt.
A Viking discovered North America.

entfalten   *to unfold*
Er entfaltet die Landkarte, um die Hauptstraße zu finden.
He unfolds the map to find the main street.

entfernen   *to remove*
Der Hautarzt entfernt ihr eine Warze.
The dermatologist removes her wart.

Entfernung(-en) f.   *distance*
Bei einer Entfernung von 300 km dauert die Reise von Wien nach
   Salzburg 3 Stunden.
*At a distance of 300 kilometers, the trip from Vienna to Salzburg takes
   3 hours.*

entführen   *to abduct*
Die Verbrecher haben den Geschäftsmann entführt.
The criminals abducted the businessman.

entgegen   *against, contrary*
Entgegen der Meinung vieler gefällt ihr die Politik der
   Regierung.
Contrary to popular opinion, she likes the government's policies.

enthüllen   *to uncover*
Die Reporterin hat den Skandal um den Politiker enthüllt.
The reporter uncovered the scandal about the politician.

entkommen   *to escape*
Er ist aus dem Gefängnis entkommen.
He escaped from prison.

entlassen   *to let go*
Er wurde von seiner Arbeit entlassen.
He was let go from his job.

entrümpeln   *to clear of junk*
Wir entrümpeln den Keller von all dem alten Zeug.
We are clearing out all the old stuff from the basement.

entschädigen   *to indemnify*
Die Versicherung entschädigt ihn für seinen Verlust.
The insurance company indemnifies him for his losses

entscheiden   *to decide*
Wir haben uns entschieden, den Urlaub in den Niederlanden zu
   verbringen.
We decided to spend our vacation in the Netherlands.

Entscheidung(-en) f.   *decision*
Es war eine gute Entscheidung, diese Aktien zu kaufen.
It was a good decision to buy these stocks.

entschließen   *to decide*
Die Familie Schuster hat sich entschlossen, nach Kanada
   auszuwandern.
The Schuster family decided to emigrate to Canada.

Entschluss(-schlüsse) m.   *decision*
So große Entschlüsse sind schwer zu treffen.
It is difficult to make such big decisions.

entschuldigen   *to excuse*
Er entschuldigt sich für sein gestriges Benehmen.
He excuses himself for his behavior yesterday.

Entschuldigung(-en) f.   *excuse*
Sie hat seine Entschuldigung angenommen.
She accepted his excuse.

entspannen   *to relax*
Am Abend entspannen sich viele vor dem Fernseher.
In the evening, many people relax in front of the TV.

Entspannung(-en) f.   *relaxation*
Der Urlaub bringt Ruhe und Entspannung.
Vacation brings peace and relaxation.

entsprechen   *to correspond to*
Es entspricht nicht der Wahrheit, was hier behauptet wird.
What is being claimed here does not correspond to the truth.

enttäuschen   *to disappoint*
Der Film hat uns sehr enttäuscht.
The movie really disappointed us.

Enttäuschung(-en) f.   *disappointment*
Die Enttäuschung war groß, wie die Mannschaft verloren hat.
The disappointment was huge when the team lost.

entwerfen   *to design*
Der Modeschöpfer entwirft ein neues Kleid.
The fashion designer designs a new dress.

entwerten   *to punch/validate a ticket*
Die Fahrkarten müssen vor Fahrtantritt entwertet werden.
Tickets must be validated before you board.

Entwerter m.   *ticket punching machine*
In jede U-Bahnhaltestelle findet man einen Entwerter.
You will find a ticket punching machine in every subway station.

entzückt   *delighted*
Von dieser Idee bin ich entzückt.
I am delighted by this idea.

erbrechen   *to vomit*
Gerhard fühlte sich krank und hat am Abend sich erbrochen.
Gerhard was feeling sick and vomited this evening.

Erdbeben n.   *earthquake*
In Deutschland und Österreich gibt es keine starken Erdbeben.
There are no strong earthquakes in Germany and Austria.

Erde f.   *earth, soil*
Er hat ein Loch in der Erde gegraben.
He dug a hole in the soil.

Erdgeschoß(-e) n.   *ground floor*
Unser Büro befindet sich im Erdgeschoß.
Our office is located on the ground floor.

erfahren   *to learn*
Ich habe soeben erfahren, dass unsere Mannschaft gewonnen hat.
I just learned that our team won.

Erfahrung(-en) f.   *experience*
Aus Erfahrung weiß sie, dass diese Reise anstrengend ist.
She knows from experience that this trip is exhausting.

erinnern   *to remember*
Er erinnert sich oft an seine Reise nach Ungarn.
He often remembers his trip to Hungary.

Erinnerung(-en) f.   *memory*
Er hat keine Erinnerung an den Unfall.
He has no memory of the accident.

Erlaubnis(-se) f.   *permission*
Er hat die Erlaubnis seiner Eltern bis Mitternacht auszubleiben.
He has his parents' permission to stay out until midnight.

ermächtigen   *to authorize*
Er ermächtigt seinen Anwalt, die Entscheidungen zu treffen.
He authorizes his attorney to make the decisions.

ernähren   *to feed*
Dieses Tier ernährt sich hauptsächlich von Pflanzen.
This animal feeds mostly on plants.

Ernährung(-en) f.   *nutrition*
Eine gute Ernährung ist wichtig für die Gesundheit.
Good nutrition is important for your health.

Ernte(-n) f.   *harvest*
Die Ernte kommt erst im Herbst.
The harvest does not start until fall.

ernten   *to harvest*
Gestern haben wir Kartoffeln geerntet.
Yesterday we harvested potatos.

erreichen   *to reach, to achieve*
In dieser Klasse haben wir viel erreicht.
We achieved a lot in this class.

errichten   *to establish*
Die Bank errichtet hier eine neue Filiale.
The bank is establishing a new branch here.

erscheinen   *to appear*
Das Buch erscheint im Herbst.
The book will come out in fall.

erschüttern   *to shock*
Die Nachrichten haben uns erschüttert.
The news shocked us.

erst   *not until*
Wir kommen erst am Dienstag in Berlin an.
We won't arrive in Berlin until Tuesday.

erstatten   *to refund*
Das Geschäft hat mir den vollen Kaufpreis für das Kleid erstattet.
The store refunded me the full sale price of the dress.

erstmals   *for the first time*
Gestern hat er erstmals den Kometen gesehen.
Yesterday he saw the comet for the first time.

Erwachsene(-n) m. and f.   *adult*
Erwachsene zahlen für den Eintritt ins Museum den vollen Preis.
Adults pay full price for museum admission.

erwarten   *to expect*
Der Flug aus Osnabrück wird für 15 Uhr erwartet.
The flight from Osnabrück is expected at 3 pm.

Erwartung(-en) f.   *expectation*
Erwartungen entsprechen nicht immer der Realität.
Expectations do not always correspond to reality.

erzählen   *to tell*
Er erzählt mir die Geschichte seines Lebens.
He tells me the story of his life

Erzähler m. **Erzählerin(-nen)** f.   *narrator*
Der Erzähler hat die Einführung zum Film gegeben.
The narrator gave the introduction to the film.

essen   *to eat*
Die Berliner essen gern Eisbein.
Berliners like to eat pork knuckles.

Essen n.   *food*
Das Essen schmeckt mir heute besonders gut.
I really enjoyed the food today.

Esszimmer n.   *dining room*
Im Esszimmer steht ein großer Tisch.
There is a large table in the dining room.

etepetete   *fussy*
Willi ist sehr etepetete, denn alles muss für ihn immer stimmen.
Willi is very fussy, as everything always has to be his way.

etwa   *about, approximately*
In etwa einer Stunde fahre ich nach Hause.
I will go home in about an hour.

etwas   *something*
Robert kauft seiner Frau etwas Schönes zum Geburtstag.
Robert is buying his wife something pretty for her birthday.

Euro m.   *euro*
Der Euro ist die Währung in Österreich und Deutschland.
The euro is the currency in Austria and Germany.

Europa n.   *Europe*
Europa ist einer von 5 Kontinenten in der Welt.
Europe is one of the world's five continents.

Europäische Union f.   *European Union*
Deutschland und Österreich sind Mitglieder der Europäischen
Union.
Germany and Austria are members of the European Union.

existieren   *to exist*
Es existiert keine Information zu diesem Thema.
There is no information on this topic.

exotisch   *exotic*
Er genießt das exotische Essen im Ausland.
He enjoys the exotic food abroad.

F

fabelhaft   *fabulous*
In diesem Restaurant haben wir ein fabelhaftes Abendessen gegessen.
We ate a fabulous dinner at this restaurant.

Fabrik(-en) f.   *factory*
In der Fabrik werden Schuhe hergestellt.
Shoes are produced in the factory.

Fach(Fächer) n.   *subject*
Welches Fach studierst du?
What subject do you study?

Fächer m.   *fan*
Im Sommer kühlt sie sich mit dem Fächer.
In summer, she cools off with a fan.

Fähre(-n) f.   *ferry*
Mit der Fähre gelangt man von Deutschland nach Schweden.
You can reach Sweden from Germany by ferry.

fahren   *to go, to drive*
Wir fahren am Wochenende aufs Land.
We are driving to the countryside on the weekend.

Fahrer m. **Fahrerin(-nen)** f.   *driver*
Der Fahrer lenkt die Straßenbahn.
The driver drives the streetcar.

Fahrkarte(-n) f.   *transit ticket*
Er hat keine Fahrkarte für die U-Bahn.
He does not have a ticket for the subway.

Fahrkartenautomat(-en) m.   *ticket vending machine*
Der Fahrkartenautomat akzeptiert Kreditkarten.
The ticket vending machine accepts credit cards.

Fall(Fälle) m.   *case*
Die Polizei hat leider viele ungelöste Fälle.
Unfortunately, the police have many unsolved cases.

Falle(-n) f.   *trap*
Er ist im Wald in eine Falle getreten.
He stepped into a trap in the woods.

fallen   *to fall*
Die Äpfel fallen aus seinen Händen.
The apples fall out of his hands.

fällig   *due*
Die Hausaufgabe ist nächste Woche fällig.
The homework is due next week.

falsch   *incorrect*
Das war die falsche Antwort auf meine Frage.
That was the incorrect answer to my question.

fangen   *to catch*
Der Junge fängt den Ball.
The boy catches the ball.

fast   *almost*
Wir haben fast genug Geld, ein neues Auto zu kaufen.
We almost have enough money to buy a new car.

fasten   *to fast*
Zu Jom Kippur müssen gläubige Juden fasten.
Observant Jews have to fast on Yom Kippur.

fechten   *to fence*
Die zwei Männer fechten zum Spaß.
The two men are fencing for fun.

Feder(-n) f.   *feather*
Die Pölster sind mit Federn gestopft.
The pillows are stuffed with feathers.

Fee(-n) f.   *fairy*
Den Kindern gefällt die gute Fee im Märchen.
The children like the good fairy in the fairy tale.

Feierabend(-e) m.   *end of work*
Nach Feierabend gehen wir noch schnell etwas essen.
After work we'll quickly get something to eat.

feiern   *to celebrate*
Wir feiern heute deinen Geburtstag.
We are celebrating your birthday today.

Feld(Felder) n.   *field*
Im Feld wachsen Sonnenblumen.
Sunflowers grow in the field.

Fenster m.   *window*
Wenn man gut isolierte Fenster im Haus hat, spart man im
   Winter beim Heizen.
*If you have well-insulated windows in your house, you'll save on
   your heating bill in winter.*

fern   *faraway*
Er reist gern in ferne Länder.
He likes to travel to faraway countries.

Fernbedienung(-en) f.   *remote control*
Mit der Fernbedienung macht er den Fernseher lauter.
He turned up the volume on the TV with the remote control.

fernsehen   *to watch TV*
Die Kinder sehen zu viel fern.
The children watch too much TV.

Fernsehen n.   *TV*
Im Fernsehen läuft nichts Interessantes.
There is nothing interesting on TV.

Fernseher m.   *TV set*
Der Fernseher ist kaputt, also müssen wir einen neuen
   kaufen.
The TV set is broken, so we have to buy a new one.

Fernsehserie(-n) f.   *TV series*
Amerikanische Fernsehserien sind in Österreich sehr beliebt.
American TV series are very popular in Austria.

fertig   *finished*
Jetzt sind wir mit dem Essen fertig.
We are finished with the meal.

fest   *tight*
Der Vater hält die Hand seiner Tochter fest.
The father holds his daughter's hand tightly.

Fest(-e) n.   *party*
Auf dem Fest waren sehr viele Gäste.
There were a lot of guests at the party.

Feuer n.   *fire*
Die Pfadfinder haben sich beim Feuer Geschichten erzählt.
The boy scouts told each other stories by the fire.

Feuerwehr(-en) f.   *fire department*
Die Feuerwehr kommt sehr schnell, wenn man sie ruft.
The fire department arrives quickly when you call them.

Fiaker m.   *horse-drawn carriage*
Die Touristen fahren gern mit dem Fiaker durch Wien.
The tourists enjoy riding in a horse-drawn carriage through Vienna.

Film(-e) m.   *movie*
Wir haben den neuen Film im Kino gesehen.
We saw the new movie at the theater.

finden   *to find*
Sie kann ihre Schlüssel nicht finden.
She can't find her keys.

Firma(Firmen) f.   *company*
Unsere Firma produziert Messer in Österreich.
Our company produces knives in Austria.

flach   *flat*
Die Landschaft von Schleswig-Holstein ist sehr flach.
Schleswig-Holstein's landscape is very flat.

Flasche(-n) f.   *bottle*
Er trinkt Wasser aus einer Flasche.
He drinks water from a bottle.

Flaschenöffner m.   *bottle opener*
Er öffnet die Flasche mit dem Flaschenöffner.
He opens the bottle with the bottle opener.

Fleet(-e) m.   *canal (in Hamburg)*
In der Stadt Hamburg gibt es viele Fleete wie die Kanäle in Venedig.
In the city of Hamburg there are many canals like in Venice.

Fleiß m.   *diligence*
Er macht seine Arbeit mit viel Fleiß.
He does his work with diligence.

fleißig   *hard working*
Die fleißigen Schüler bekommen bessere Noten.
Hard-working students get better grades.

fliegen   *to fly*
Nächste Woche fliegen die Schneiders nach Australien, um ihre
   Verwandten zu besuchen.
Next week the Schneiders will fly to Australia to visit their relatives.

fließen   *to flow*
Die Donau fließt ins Schwarze Meer.
The Danube flows into the Black Sea.

Flöte(-n) f.   *flute*
Das Mädchen spielt ein Lied auf der Flöte.
The girl plays a song on the flute.

fluchen   *to curse*
Er flucht auf die neuen Preiserhöhungen.
He curses at the new price increases.

flüchten   *to flee*
Diese Familie ist nach Deutschland geflohen.
The family fled to Germany.

Flüchtling(-e) m.   *refugee*
Er ist ein Flüchtling aus dem Bürgerkrieg.
He is a refugee of the civil war.

Flug(Flüge) m.   *flight*
Der Flug nach Izmir dauert 3 Stunden.
The flight to Izmir lasts 3 hours.

Flügel m.   *wing*
Der Vogel hat einen gebrochenen Flügel.
The bird has a broken wing.

Flughafen(-häfen) m.   *airport*
Am Flughafen gibt es mehrere Restaurants.
There are several restaurants at the airport.

Fluglinie(-n) f.   *airline*
In Deutschland gibt es mehrere Fluglinien.
There are several airlines in Germany.

Flugsteig(-e) m.   *airport gate*
Der Flug nach Genf geht von Flugsteig 21 ab.
The flight to Geneva departs from gate 21.

Flugzeug(-e) n.   *airplane*
Der Airbus 380 ist das größte Passagierflugzeug in der Welt.
The Airbus 380 is the largest passenger airplane in the world.

Fluss(Flüsse) m.   *river*
Der Rhein und die Donau sind die bekanntesten Flüsse im
  deutschsprachigen Europa.
*The Rhine and the Danube are the most well-known rivers in German-
  speaking Europe.*

flüstern   *to whisper*
Er flüstert ihr ein Geheimnis ins Ohr.
He whispers a secret into her ear.

Flut(-en) f.   *flood*
Die Flut hat an der Nordseeküste zahlreiche Schäden
  verursacht.
The flood caused numerous damages on the North Sea coast.

Föhn(-e) m.   *hair dryer*
Sie trocknet die Haare mit einem Föhn.
She dries her hair with a hair dryer.

fördern   *to encourage*
Der Lehrer fördert seine Schüler.
The teacher encourages his students.

fordern   *to demand*
Der Kanzler fordert höhere Steuern.
The chancellor demands higher taxes.

Foto(-s) n.   *photo*
Das ist ein schönes Foto von dir.
This is a nice photo of you.

fotografieren   *to take a picture*
Sie fotografiert das Brandenburger Tor.
She takes a picture of the Brandenburg Gate.

Frage(-n) f.   *question*
Die Schüler haben heute in der Klasse viele Fragen gestellt.
The students asked many questions in class today.

fragen   *to ask*
Er fragt sie nach der genauen Uhrzeit.
He asks her for the exact time.

Franken m.   *franc*
In der Schweiz bezahlt man in Franken.
You pay with francs in Switzerland.

Frankreich n.   *France*
Frankreich ist ein Land in Westeuropa.
France is a country in Western Europe.

Franzose(-n) m. **Französin(-nen)** f.   *French person*
Michel ist Franzose und kommt aus Lyon.
Michel is French and comes from Lyon.

französisch   *French*
In Deutschland isst man gern französischen Käse.
In Germany, people like to eat French cheeses.

Frau(-en) f.   *lady, Ms.*
Frau Schmidt wohnt in der Kärntnerstraße.
Ms. Schmidt lives on Kärntner Street.

Fräulein n.   *miss*
Entschuldigen Sie Fräulein, wo finde ich die nächste Apotheke?
Excuse me miss, where can I find the nearest pharmacy?

frech   *sassy, fresh*
Die Kinder waren heute wieder frech und haben viel Lärm
   gemacht.
The children were sassy again today and made a lot of noise.

Frechheit(-en) f.   *insolence, nerve*
Das ist aber eine Frechheit!
What nerve!

frei   *free*
In der Garage gibt es noch einige freie Stellplätze.
The are still a few free parking spaces in the garage.

Freiheit(-en) f.   *freedom*
Die Freiheit ist ein wichtiges Grundrecht unserer Gesellschaft.
Freedom is an important fundamental right in our society.

fressen   *to devour, to eat (used with animals)*
Die Schweine fressen aus dem Trog im Stall.
The pigs are eating from the trough in the stable.

Freund(-e) m. **Freundin(-nen)** f.   *friend*
Florian geht mit seiner Freundin ins Kino.
Florian is going with his girlfriend to the movies.

freundlich   *friendly*
Die Ärzte im Krankenhaus waren sehr freundlich.
The doctors in the hospital were very friendly.

Freundschaft(-en) f.   *friendship*
Diese Freundschaft existiert schon seit Jahren.
This friendship has existed for years.

Frieden m.   *peace*
Auf den Krieg folgt der Frieden.
War is followed by peace.

Friedhof(-höfe) m.   *cemetery*
Auf dem Friedhof steht eine kleine Kapelle.
There is a small chapel in the cemetery.

frisch   *fresh*
Ich esse gern frische Fische.
I like to eat fresh fish.

Frische f.   *freshness*
Er genießt die Frische der Seeluft.
He enjoys the freshness of the sea breeze.

frisieren   *to comb*
Sie frisiert sich die Haare.
She is combing her hair.

Frisur(-en) f.   *hairdo*
Frau Markl hat diese Woche eine neue Frisur.
Ms. Markl has a new hairdo this week.

froh   *happy, merry*
Frohes Fest!
Happy Holidays!

fröhlich   *cheerful*
Die Kinder singen fröhliche Lieder.
The children sing cheerful songs.

Fröhlichkeit(-en) f.   *cheerfulness*
Wir brauchen mehr Fröhlichkeit.
We need more cheerfulness.

fromm   *pious*
Er ist sehr fromm und geht am Sonntag zur Kirche.
He is very pious and goes to church on Sunday.

früh   *early*
Istvan steht sehr früh auf und geht zur Arbeit.
Istvan gets up very early and goes to work.

Frühstück(-e) n.   *breakfast*
Frühstück ist viel bescheidener als in England.
Breakfast in Germany is much more modest than in England.

frühstücken   *to eat breakfast*
Die Familie frühstückt jeden Morgen gemeinsam.
The family eats breakfast together every morning.

fühlen   *to feel*
Er fühlt die kalte Luft auf seinem Gesicht.
He feels the cold air on his face.

führen   *to lead*
Frau Harell führt ihre Klasse in den Zoo.
Ms. Harell leads her class to the zoo.

Führerschein(-e) m.   *driver's licence*
Ohne Führerschein darf man kein Auto fahren.
You are not allowed to drive a car without a driver's licence.

Führung(-en) f.   *guided tour*
Der Gruppe hat die Führung durch das Schloss gefallen.
The group enjoyed the guided tour through the palace.

füllen   *to fill*
Er füllt den Tank mit Benzin.
He fills the tank with gasoline.

Füllfeder(-n) f.   *fountain pen*
In Österreich schreiben die Volksschüler mit Füllfeder.
In Austria, elementary school students write with a fountain pen.

für   *for*
Diese Karte ist für Sie.
This card is for you.

fürchten   *to be afraid*
Sie fürchtet sich vor Gespenstern.
She is afraid of ghosts.

Fürst(-en) m.   *prince*
Der Fürst ist das Staatsoberhaupt des Fürstentum Liechtenstein.
The prince is the head of state of the Principality of Liechtenstein.

Fürstentum(-tümer) n.   *principality*
Im Heiligen Römischen Reich gab es mehrere deutsche
Fürstentümer.
*There were several German principalities in the Holy Roman
Empire.*

Fußball(-bälle) m.   *soccer (ball)*
Der Junge hat seinen Fußball verloren.
The boy lost his soccer ball.

Fußball spielen   *to play soccer*
Die Jugendlichen spielen Fußball im Park.
The teenagers play soccer in the park.

Fußgänger m. **Fußgängerin(-nen)** f.   *pedestrian*
Die Fußgänger spazieren in der Stadt.
The pedestrians are going for a walk in the city.

Fußgängerzone(-n) f.   *pedestrian zone*
Die Münchner Kaufingerstraße ist eine Fußgängerzone, und da
dürfen keine Autos fahren.
*Munich's Kaufinger Street is a pedestrian zone, and no cars are allowed
there.*

Futter n.   *feed*
Der Bauer gibt den Tieren Futter.
The farmer gives feed to his animals.

füttern   *to feed*
Die Mutter füttert ihr Kind.
The mother feeds her child.

G

Gabel(-n) f.   *fork*
Er isst die Nudeln mit einer Gabel.
He eats the noodles with a fork.

Gabelfrühstück(-e) n.   *second breakfast*
Jeden Tag um 10 Uhr isst Herr Pollak sein Gabelfrühstück.
Every day at 10 o'clock, Mr. Pollak eats his second breakfast.

ganz   *whole, very*
Wir sind ganz zufrieden mit unserem Wagen.
We are very pleased with our car.

Garage(-n) f.　*garage*
Autos kann man in einer Garage parken.
You can park cars in a garage.

Garantie(-n) f.　*guarantee*
Dieser Kühlschrank kommt mit einer einjährigen Garantie.
This refrigerator comes with a one-year guarantee.

Garten(Gärten) m.　*garden*
Im Garten stehen zwei große Bäume.
There are two large trees in the yard.

Gas n.　*natural gas*
Wir heizen mit Gas.
We heat with natural gas.

Gasse(-n) f.　*alley, small street*
In dieser Gasse finden Sie zwei kleine Geschäfte.
You will find two small stores in this alley.

Gast(Gäste) m.　*guest*
Die Gäste sind mit dem Hotel sehr zufrieden.
The guests are very satisfied with the hotel.

Gasthaus(-häuser) n.　*restaurant, inn*
Wir essen das Abendessen im Gasthaus.
We are eating dinner at the inn.

Gauner m.　*crook*
Der Gauner hat das Fahrrad gestohlen.
The crook stole the bike.

Gebäude n.　*building*
Das Gebäude wird von unserer Firma geputzt.
The building is being cleaned by our company.

geben　*give*
Sie gibt ihm 5 Euro, damit er Mineralwasser kauft.
She gives him 5 euros to buy mineral water.

Gebiet(-e) n.　*territory*
In diesem Gebiet darf nicht gejagt werden.
Hunting is not allowed in this territory.

Geburtstag(-e) m.　*birthday*
Veronika hat im Juli ihren 6. Geburtstag.
Veronika has her sixth birthday in July.

Geburtstagsfeier(-n) f.   *birthday party*
Die Familie hat dem Großvater eine schöne Geburtstagsfeier
    bereitet.
The family prepared a nice birthday party for the grandfather.

gedenken   *commemorate*
Am 9. November gedenken die Deutschen der
    Reichspogromnacht.
Germans commemorate the Night of Broken Glass on November 9.

Gedenkstätte(-n) f.   *memorial*
In Deutschland und Österreich gibt es mehrere Gedenkstätten
    für die Opfer des Nationalsozialismus.
In Germany and Austria, there are several memorials for Nazi victims.

Gedicht(-e) n.   *poem*
Die Kinder lesen ein Gedicht von Paul Celan.
The children read a poem by Paul Celan.

Gefahr(-en) f.   *danger*
Sie befinden sich in Gefahr.
You are in danger.

gefährlich   *dangerous*
Das ist eine gefährliche Straße, auf der viele Unfälle passieren.
This is a dangerous street, as many accidents happen on it.

gefallen   *to like*
Mir gefällt dein neues Hemd.
I like your new shirt.

Gefallen m.   *favor*
Könntest du mir einen Gefallen tun und heute auf die Kinder
    aufpassen?
Could you do me a favor and watch my children today?

Gefängnis(-e) n.   *prison*
Verbrecher werden im Gefängnis eingesperrt.
Criminals are locked up in prison.

Gefühl(-e) n.   *feeling*
Er hat kein gutes Gefühl über das Projekt.
He does not have a good feeling about the project.

gegen   *against*
Herr Lingen ist gegen die neue Initiative.
Mr. Lingen is against the new initiative.

geheim *secret*
Wir brauchen Informationen aus der geheimen Akte.
We need information from the secret file.

Geheimnis(-se) n. *secret*
Sie hat ein Geheimnis, das sie niemanden erzählt.
She has a secret that she won't tell anyone.

gehen *to go, to walk*
Wir gehen in den Park.
We are walking to the park.

gehören *to belong to*
Das schöne Buch gehört Frau Gradwohl.
That lovely book belongs to Ms. Gradwohl.

Gehsteig(-e) m. *sidewalk*
Die Fußgänger gehen auf dem Gehsteig.
The pedestrians walk on the sidewalk.

Geige(-n) f. *violin*
Franz spielt ein Lied auf der Geige.
Franz is playing a song on the violin.

Geist(-er) m. *ghost*
Der Geist spukt im Schloss.
The ghost haunts the palace.

gelangen *to reach*
Mit der Straßenbahn gelangt man in die Innenstadt.
You can reach downtown by streetcar.

Geld(-er) n. *money*
Er hat kein Geld auf der Bank.
He has no money in the bank.

Geldbörse(-n) f. *wallet*
Seine Geldbörse steckt in einer Hosentasche.
His wallet is in his pants pocket.

Geldschein(-e) m. *paper money bill*
Er wechselt den Geldschein in Münzen.
He changes the paper bills into coins.

Gelegenheit(-en) f. *opportunity*
Ich freue mich auf die Gelegenheit, nach Australien zu fahren.
I am looking forward to the opportunity to travel to Australia.

Gemälde n.   *painting*
Viele Gemälde hängen in der Gallerie.
There are many paintings in the gallery.

gemein   *mean*
Das ist ein gemeines Kind, dass nicht gern mit anderen
Kindern spielt.
*This is a mean child that does not like to play with other
children.*

gemeinsam   *together*
Wir fahren dieses Jahr gemeinsam in Urlaub.
We will be going on vacation together this year.

Gemeinschaft(-en) f.   *community*
Er arbeitet für die Gemeinschaft.
He works for the community.

gemütlich   *cozy*
Wir sitzen gemütlich beim Heurigen.
We are very cozy sitting at the wine bar.

Gemütlichkeit(-en) f.   *coziness, warmth and friendliness*
Gemütlichkeit ist ein Teil österreichischer Lebenskultur.
Warmth and friendliness are a part of Austrian culture.

genädig   *gracious*
Sie war so genädig, uns die Wohnung für eine Woche zu
überlassen.
She was gracious enough to give us the apartment for a week.

genießen   *to savor*
Er genießt die wunderbaren Speisen in diesem Restaurant.
He savors the wonderful dishes at this restaurant.

genieren   *to be ashamed*
Udo geniert sich, vor seinen Freunden zu singen.
Udo is ashamed to sing in front of his friends.

Genuss(-nüsse) m.   *consumption*
Der Genuss von Zigaretten ist hier verboten.
Cigarette consumption is prohibited here.

Gepäck n.   *luggage*
Am Flughafen gibt er sein Gepäck auf.
He checks in his luggage at the airport.

gerade   *straight*
Er steht gerade.
He is standing up straight.

geradeaus   *straight ahead*
Das Rathaus befindet sich geradeaus.
City hall is straight ahead.

Gericht(-e) n.   *court of law*
Auf dem Gericht wird ein Fall verhandelt.
A case is being judged in court.

gering   *small*
Die Rentnerin hat nur ein geringes Einkommen.
The retired woman only has a small income.

geringfügig   *marginal, minimal*
Dieser geringfügiger Betrag muss nicht versteuert werden.
Such a minimal amount does not have to be taxed.

gern   *with pleasure, to like to*
Ferdinand spielt gern Golf mit seinen Freunden.
Ferdinand likes to play golf with his friends.

Gerücht(-e) n.   *rumor*
Ein böses Gerücht ist in der Luft.
There is a bad rumor in the air.

Gesang(Gesänge) m.   *singing*
Ihr gefällt der Gesang des Chors.
She likes the choir's singing.

Geschäft(-e) n.   *store, business*
Die Familie besitzt ein Geschäft in Genf.
The family owns a store in Geneva.

Geschäftsreise(-n) f.   *business trip*
Herr Novak ist auf Geschäftsreise in Aserbaidschan.
Mr. Novak is on a business trip in Azerbaijan.

Geschenk(-e) n.   *gift*
Zum Geburtstag bekommt sie ein Geschenk.
She gets a gift on her birthday.

Geschenkpapier(-e) n.   *wrapping paper*
Die Überraschung wickelt er in Geschenkpapier.
He wraps the surprise in wrapping paper.

Geschichte(-n) f.   *story, history*
Die Großmutter erzählt den Kindern eine Geschichte aus ihrer Jugend.
The grandmother tells the children a story from her youth.

Geschirr n.   *table settings, dishes*
Das Geschirr wird in der Spülmaschine gewaschen.
The dishes are being washed in the dishwasher.

Geschmack m.   *taste, flavor*
Mir gefällt der Geschmack von Knoblauch.
I like the flavor of garlic.

geschmacklos   *tasteless*
Diese geschmacklose Geste solltest du nicht wiederholen.
You should not repeat such a tasteless gesture.

gesegnet   *blessed*
Der Pfarrer hat das Kind gesegnet.
The priest blessed the child.

Gesellschaft(-en) f.   *society*
Wir leben in einer demokratischen Gesellschaft.
We live in a democratic society.

Gesetz(-e) n.   *law*
Gesetze sind von Land zu Land unterschiedlich.
Laws are different from one country to another.

Gesetzgebung(-en) f.   *legislation*
Die Gesetzgebung dieses Landes verbietet solche Handlungen.
The legislation of this country prohibits such actions.

Gespenst(-er) n.   *ghost*
Gespenster gibt es in Wirklichkeit nicht.
Ghosts do not really exist.

Gespräch(-e) m.   *conversation*
Er führt ein Gespräch mit einem Kunden.
He is carrying on a conversation with a customer.

gestern   *yesterday*
Gestern war das Wetter nicht so schön wie heute.
The weather was not as nice yesterday as it is today.

gesund   *healthy*
Eine gesunde Ernährung ist für den Körper sehr wichtig.
A healthy diet is very important for the body.

Gesundheit f.   *health*
Die Gesundheit ist das wichtigste im Leben.
Health is the most important thing in life.

Getränk(-e) n.   *drink*
Im Supermarkt kann man Getränke kaufen.
You can buy drinks at the grocery store.

Getreide n.   *silage, grain*
In der Lagerhalle lagert das Getreide.
The grain is stored in the warehouse.

Gewerkschaft(-en) f.   *labor union*
Die Gewerkschaften spielen eine große Rolle in der deutschen
  Innenpolitik.
Labor unions play a large roll in German domestic politics.

gewiss   *certain*
Das Wetter wird morgen gewiss besser.
The weather will certainly be better tomorrow.

Gewissen n.   *conscience*
Er hat ein schlechtes Gewissen, weil er keine gute Arbeit
  geleistet hat.
He has a guilty conscience, because he did not do a good job.

gewöhnen   *to get used to*
Ich gewöhne mich an das warme Klima am Mittelmeer.
I am getting used to the warm climate in the Mediterranean.

gewöhnlich   *usually*
Herr Schwarz geht gewöhnlich am Sonntag in die Kirche.
Mr. Schwarz usually goes to church on Sunday.

Gewürz(-e) n.   *spice*
Sie kocht gern mit Gewürzen.
She likes to cook with spices.

Gier f.   *greed*
Er hat aus Gier das Geld gestohlen.
He stole the money out of greed.

gierig   *greedy*
Er ist sehr gierig und gönnt sich nie etwas.
He is very greedy and never indulges in anything.

gießen   *to pour water*
Wenn es trocken ist, muss man die Pflanzen gießen.
When it is dry, you need to water the plants.

Gießkanne(-n) f.   *watering can*
Er nimmt die Gießkanne mit in den Garten.
He takes the watering can with him to the garden.

Gift(-e) n.   *poison*
Das Gift dieser Schlange ist sehr gefährlich.
This snake's poison is very dangerous.

giftig   *poisonous*
Manche Pilze sind giftig.
Some mushrooms are poisonous.

Gitarre(-n) f.   *guitar*
Sie spielt ein Lied auf der Gitarre.
She plays a song on her guitar.

Glas(Gläser) n.   *glass*
Er erhebt sein Glas und prostet auf die Gesundheit seines
    Freundes.
He raises his glass and toasts to the health of his friend.

Glatteis n.   *black ice*
Bei Glatteis muss man vorsichtig gehen, um nicht
    auszurutschen.
When there black ice, you need to walk carefully so you don't slip.

glauben   *to believe*
Ich glaube, dass es morgen regnen wird.
I believe that it will rain tomorrow.

gleich   *same*
Die zwei Damen haben das gleiche Kleid auf dem Ball getragen.
The two ladies wore the same dress to the ball.

Gleichheit(-en) f.   *equality*
Die Gleichheit von Mann und Frau ist ein Grundprinzip unserer
    Gesellschaft.
Gender equality is a basic principle of our society.

Gleis(-e) n.   *railroad track*
Der Zug nach Görlitz fährt auf Gleis 4 ein.
The train to Görlitz is arriving at track 4.

Glück n. *luck*
Der Lehrer wünscht der Klasse viel Glück bei der Prüfung.
The teacher wishes the class good luck on the exam.

glücklich *happy*
Ich bin so glücklich, dass mein Freund die Operation gut
  überstanden hat.
I am so happy that my friend got through the surgery well.

Glückwunsch(-wünsche) m. *best wishes, congratulations*
Anläßlich Ihres Geburtstages übermittle ich Ihnen die
  Glückwünsche aller KollegInnen.
I am conveying hapy birthday wishes from all your colleagues.

Glühbirne(-n) f. *light bulb*
Wenn eine Glühbirne ausbrennt, muss man sie auswechseln.
When a light bulb burns out, it needs to be changed.

Glühwein(-e) m. *mulled wine*
Bei jedem Weihnachtsmarkt findet man Glühwein.
At every Christmas market you will find mulled wine.

Gold n. *gold*
Manche Leute investieren in Gold.
Some people invest in gold.

Gott m. *God*
Religiöse Menschen glauben an Gott
Religious people believe in God.

Grab(Gräber) n. *grave*
Auf dem Friedhof stehen viele Gräber aus dem 19. Jahrhundert.
There are many graves from the 19th century in the cemetery.

Grabstein(-e) m. *tombstone*
Sie hat für das Grab einen schönen Grabstein aus Marmor
  gekauft.
She bought a nice marble tombstone for the grave.

grantig *cranky*
Er hat heute eine schlechte Laune und daher ist er grantig.
He is in a bad mood today and that is why he is cranky.

Gras(Gräser) n. *grass*
Friedl mäht das Gras im Garten.
Friedl mows the lawn.

gratis   *free of charge*
Der Eintritt ins Museum ist gratis.
Museum admission is free of charge.

grauenhaft   *terrible*
Das war ein grauenhaftes Hotel, weil sie die Zimmer nicht
   geputzt haben.
This was a terrible hotel because they did not clean the rooms.

grausam   *cruel*
Der grausame Verbrecher wurde von der Polizei geschnappt.
The cruel criminal was caught by the police.

greifen   *to reach*
Er greift nach dem Salz auf dem Tisch.
He reaches for the salt on the table.

Grenze(-n) f.   *border*
An der Grenze werden die Pässe kontrolliert.
The passports are checked at the border.

grenzen   *to border*
Österreich grenzt an Ungarn.
Austria borders Hungary.

groß   *big, large*
Dieses Flugzeug hat die größten Flügel, die ich je gesehen habe.
This airplane has the largest wings that I have ever seen.

Größe(-n) f.   *size*
Ist das die richtige Größe für das Kleid?
Is this the right size for the dress?

Großherzog(-e) m.   *grand duke*
Der Großherzog ist das Staatsoberhaupt von Luxemburg.
The grand duke is the head of state in Luxembourg.

Großherzogtum(-tümer) n.   *grand duchy*
Luxemburg ist ein Großherzogtum.
Luxembourg is a grand duchy.

Gruß(Grüße) m.   *greeting*
Aus dem Urlaub sende ich liebe Grüße an die ganze Familie.
I send dear greetings to the whole family while on vacation.

grüßen   *to greet*
Das ist ein freundliches Mädchen, das alle Nachbarn nett grüßt.
She is a friendly girl who kindly greets all her neighbors.

Gummistiefel m. *rubber boots*
Bei Regenwetter trägt sie gern Gummistiefel.
She likes to wear rubber boots in rainy weather.

gut *good*
Johann ist ein guter Junger.
Johann is a good boy.

Gut(Güter) n. *estate*
Es gibt drei Ställe auf dem Gut.
There are three stables on the estate.

Gutschein(-e) m. *coupon*
Mit diesem Gutschein bekomme ich 20% Rabatt.
I get 20% off with this coupon.

Gymnasium(Gymnasien) n. *high school*
Wenn man in Deutschland studieren will, muss man zuerst aufs
Gymnasium gehen.
If you want to study in Germany, you have to go to high school first.

H

Haarspange(-n) f. *barrette*
Sie gibt eine Haarspange in die Haare.
She puts a barrette in her hair.

haben *to have*
Elfriede hat zwei Bäume in ihrem Garten.
Elfriede has two trees in her yard.

Hafen(Häfen) m. *harbor*
Das Schiff ist vor zwei Stunden im Hafen angekommen.
The ship arrived in the harbor two hours ago.

häkeln *to crochet*
Sie häkelt einen roten Schal für ihren Bruder.
She is crocheting a red scarf for her brother.

Haken m. *hook*
Häng deine Jacke bitte an den Haken.
Please hang your jacket on the hook.

halb *half*
Das Glas ist noch halb voll.
The glass is still half full.

Halbinsel(-n) f.   *peninsula*
Italien ist eine Halbinsel in Europa.
Italy is a peninsula in Europe.

Hälfte(-n) f.   *half*
Das ist meine Hälfte des Gewinn.
This is my half of the earnings.

halten   *to hold*
Er halt ein Buch in der Hand.
He is holding a book in his hand.

Haltestelle(-n) f.   *public transit stop*
Bitte steigen Sie bei dieser Haltestelle aus.
Please get off at this stop.

Hammer(Hämmer) m.   *hammer*
Er schlägt einen Nagel mit dem Hammer ein.
He hits a nail with the hammer.

Handbuch(-bücher) n.   *handbook*
Die Regeln findest du im Handbuch.
You will find the rules in the handbook.

Handlung(-en) f.   *action*
Die Handlungen des Mannes haben viele beunruhigt.
The man's actions worried many people.

Handtasche(-n) f.   *purse*
Frau Rütli hat ihre Handtasche in der Konditorei vergessen.
Ms. Rütli forgot her purse in the pastry shop.

Handy(-s) n.   *cell phone*
Du kannst mich jederzeit auf meinem Handy anrufen.
You can call me anytime on my cell phone.

Hass m.   *hatred*
Er ist ein trauriger Mensch, der zu viel Hass hat.
He is a sad person who has too much hatred.

hässlich   *ugly*
Das ist eine hässliche Puppe, die mir nicht gefällt.
This is an ugly doll that I do not like.

hauptsächlich   *mainly*
Er arbeitet hauptsächlich an der Universität.
He works mainly at the university.

Hauptstadt(-städte) f.   *capital*
Bern ist die Hauptstadt der Schweiz.
Bern is the capital of Switzerland.

Haus(Häuser) n.   *house*
Herr Müller kauft sein erstes Haus.
Mr. Müller is buying his first house.

Hausarbeit(-en) f.   *homework*
Die Lehrerin hat den Schülern viel Hausarbeit gegeben.
The teacher gave the students lots of homework.

heben   *to lift*
Er hebt die Hand und zeigt auf das Auto.
He lifts his hand and points to the car.

Heft(-e) n.   *notebook*
Sie macht Notizen in kleines blaues Heft.
She is taking notes in a small blue notebook.

heften   *to staple*
Sie heftet die Seiten zusammen.
She staples the pages together.

heikel   *delicate, tricky*
Das ist ein heikles Thema, das man nicht vor den Kindern
    besprechen sollte.
This is a delicate topic that should not be discussed in front of children.

heilen   *to heal*
Die Wunde war nicht so schlimm und heilte innerhalb einer
    Woche.
The wound wasn't that bad and healed within a week.

heilig   *holy*
Der heilige Florian ist der Schutzpatron der Feuerwehr in
    Österreich.
Holy Florian is the patron saint of fire departments in Austria.

Heilige(-n) m./f.   *saint*
In der katholischen Kirche gibt es viele Heilige.
There are many saints in the Catholic Church.

Heimat f.   *homeland*
John kommt aus Seattle und seine Heimat ist Amerika.
John is from Seattle and his homeland is the United States.

Heimweh n.   *homesickness*
Hans hat Heimweh nach Österreich.
Hans is homesick for Austria.

Heirat(-en) f.   *marriage*
Diese Heirat war sehr kurz und hat nur fünf Jahre gedauert.
The marriage was very short and lasted only five years.

heiraten   *to marry*
Dieses Paar hat in der Kirche geheiratet.
This couple got married in the church.

heiß   *hot*
Dieser Kaffee ist zu heiß für mich, und ich muss warten,
   bis er abkühlt.
This coffee is too hot for me and I need to wait until it cools down.

heißen   *to be called*
Sie heißt Susanne.
She is called Susanne.

heizen   *to heat*
Früher hat man in Deutschland mit Kohle geheizt.
In the past, people in Germany used to heat with coal.

helfen   *to help*
Der Junge hilft einer älteren Dame über die Straße.
The boy helps an elderly lady cross the street.

hell   *bright*
Bitte, zieh die Vorhänge zu, denn es ist hell in diesem Zimmer.
Please shut the curtains because it is bright in this room.

Herd(-e) m.   *stove*
Das Wasser kocht auf dem Herd.
The water is boiling on the stove.

Herkunft(-künfte) f.   *origin*
Die Herkunft des Pakets ist unbekannt.
The package's origin is unknown.

Herr(-en) m.   *gentleman, Mr.*
Fragen Sie doch den Herrn dort drüben.
Go and ask the gentleman over there.

herrlich   *wonderful*
Dieser herrliche Film hat allen gefallen.
Everyone liked this wonderful film.

herrschen   *to rule*
Der Kaiser hat über ein großes Reich geherrscht.
The emperor ruled over a vast empire.

herstellen   *to produce*
In Deutschland werden viele Autos hergestellt.
Many cars are produced in Germany.

hervorragend   *outstanding*
In diesem Restaurant haben wir eine hervorragende Suppe
    gegessen.
We ate an outstanding soup at this restaurant.

heulen   *to cry*
Die Kinder heulen aus Trauer.
The children cry out of grief.

Heurige(-n) m.   *wine restaurant (in Vienna)*
In Wien findet man viele gemütliche Heurigen.
You will find many cozy wine bars in Vienna.

heute   *today*
Heute ist das Wetter aber schön.
The weather is really nice today.

Hexe(-n) f.   *witch*
Die böse Hexe hat die Kinder in ihr Häuschen gelockt.
The evil witch lured the children into her house.

hier   *here*
Ich wohne hier seit fünf Jahren.
I have lived here for five years.

Hinweis(-e) m.   *clue, tip*
Die Polizei wartet auf Hinweise aus der Bevölkerung.
The police are waiting for tips from the public.

Hitze(-n) f.   *heat*
Die Hitze war diesen Sommer sehr anstrengend und daher haben
    wir eine Klimaanlage gekauft.
*The heat was exhausting this summer and that is why we bought an air
    conditioner.*

hoch   *high*
Der Ritter sitzt hoch auf dem Pferd.
The knight sits high on the horse.

Hochzeit(-en) f.   *wedding*
Auf der Hochzeit haben viele der Gäste getanzt.
Many of the guests danced at the wedding.

hocken   *to crouch*
Er hockt auf dem Boden.
He is crouching on the floor.

Hocker m.   *stool*
Ernst sitzt auf einem Hocker in der Küche.
Ernst sits on a stool in the kitchen.

Hof(Höfe) m.   *courtyard*
Im Hof ist genug Platz, zwei Autos zu parken.
There is enough room in the courtyard to park two cars.

hoffen   *to hope*
Sie hoffen noch immer auf ein Wunder.
They are still hoping for a miracle.

Hoffnung(-en) f.   *hope*
Es ist wichtig, nie die Hoffnung zu verlieren.
It is important to never lose hope.

höflich   *polite*
Frau Schatzinger ist sehr höflich, weil sie ihre Nachbarn immer
  grüßt.
*Ms. Schatzinger is very polite because she always greets her
  neighbors.*

Höhe(-n) f.   *height*
Der LKW hat eine Höhe von 2,5 Metern.
The truck has a height of 2.5 meters.

Höhle(-n) f.   *cave*
Der Bär schläft in einer Höhle.
The bear is sleeping in a cave.

holen   *to fetch*
Er hollt sich einen Imbiss aus der Küche.
He fetches a snack from the kitchen.

Hölle(-n) f.   *hell*
Diese Reise war die Hölle, weil alles schief gegangen ist.
This trip was hell because everything went wrong.

Holocaust m. *Holocaust*
Im Holocaust haben die Nazis 6 Millionen jüdische Europäer
ermordet.
*The Nazis murdered six million Jewish Europeans during the
Holocaust.*

Holz(Hölzer) n. *wood*
Viele Häuser in Schweden sind aus Holz.
Many houses in Sweden are made of wood.

Holzlöffel m. *wooden spoon*
In der Salatschüssel ist ein Holzlöffel.
There is a wooden spoon in the salad bowl.

Hotel(-s) n. *hotel*
Wenn ich reise, steige ich gern in einem guten Hotel ab.
I like to stay at a good hotel when I travel.

hübsch *pretty*
Das ist ein hübsches Kleid, dass du zum Ball tragen solltest.
This is a pretty dress that you should wear to the ball.

husten *to cough*
Er ist krank und hustet viel.
He is sick and coughs a lot.

I

Idee(-n) f. *idea*
Das ist eine gute Idee von dir.
That is a good idea you have.

ignorieren *to ignore*
Er hat das Problem zuerst ignoriert und jetzt ist es ein größeres
Problem.
He ignored the problem at first and now it is an even bigger problem.

Imbiss(-e) m. *snack*
Jeden Morgen gegen 10 Uhr isst er einen Imbiss.
Every morning around 10 am he eats a snack.

immer *always*
Sie ist immer glücklich.
She is always happy.

impfen   *to vaccinate*
Er lässt sich gegen Grippe impfen.
He is getting vaccinated against the flu.

Impfung(-en) f.   *vaccination*
Der Arzt gibt dem Patienten eine Impfung.
The doctor gives the patient a vaccination.

in   *in*
Er sitzt in der Straßenbahn.
He is sitting in the streetcar.

infizieren   *to infect*
Krankenpfleger tragen Handschuhe, um sich nicht mit
    Krankheiten zu infizieren.
Nurses wear gloves so they are not infected with diseases.

Inhalt(-e) m.   *content*
Der Inhalt des Buches hat mir sehr gefallen.
I really liked the book's content.

Initiative(-n) f.   *initiative*
Ich unterstützte die Initiative des Politikers.
I support the politician's initiative.

innen   *inside*
Die Tür befindet sich innen.
The door is inside.

Innenstadt(-städte) f.   *downtown*
Wien hat eine herrliche Innenstadt.
Vienna has a wonderful downtown.

Insel(-n) f.   *island*
Helgoland ist ein deutsche Insel in der Nordsee.
Heligoland is a German island in the North Sea.

intelligent   *intelligent*
Das ist ein intelligenter Mensch, der acht Sprachen spricht.
That is an intelligent person who speaks eight languages.

interessant   *interesting*
Gestern habe ich eine interessante Geschichte über den König
    von Spanien gehört.
Yesterday I heard an interesting story about the king of Spain.

Interesse(-n) n. *interest*
Er hat Interesse am Kauf eines Motorrads.
He has interest in buying a motorcycle.

interessieren *to be interested in*
Er interessiert sich für andere Kulturen.
He is interested in different cultures.

Internat(-e) n. *boarding school*
Sie hat als Mädchen ein Internat besucht.
She attended a boarding school when she was a girl.

international *international*
Diese internationale Brücke verbindet Deutschland mit der Schweiz.
This international bridge connects Germany with Switzerland.

Intrige(-n) f. *intrigue*
Er ist das Opfer einer Intrige.
He is the victim of an intrigue.

irgendwann *sometime*
Irgendwann sehen wir uns wieder.
We'll see each other again sometime.

irgendwas *something*
Ich möchte irgendwas kaufen.
I want to buy something.

irgendwo *somewhere*
Er verbringt seinen Urlaub irgendwo in Griechenland.
He is spending his vacation somewhere in Greece.

irren *to be wrong*
Entschuldigung! Ich habe mich in der Nummer geirrt.
Excuse me! I have the wrong phone number.

Islam m. *Islam*
Der Islam ist eine der wichtigsten Religionen der Welt.
Islam is one of the most important religions in the world.

Israel n. *Israel*
Israel ist ein Land im Mittelmeerraum.
Israel is a country in the Mediterranean.

Israeli(-s) m. **Israelin(-nen)** f. *Israeli*
Herr Nagy ist Israeli und kommt aus Tel Aviv.
Mr. Nagy is an Israeli who comes from Tel Aviv.

J

ja   *yes*
Ja, das stimmt absolut.
Yes, that is absolutely correct.

jagen   *to hunt*
Die Jäger jagen Wildschweine im Wald.
The hunters hunt wild boars in the forest.

jammern   *to whine*
Er jammert über seine Probleme.
He is whining about his problems.

jäten   *to weed*
Kati jätet Unkraut in ihrem Garten.
Kati is weeding weeds in her garden.

Jause(-n) f.   *afternoon snack*
Um 16 Uhr gibt es bei uns immer eine gute Jause.
We always have a good afternoon snack at 4 pm.

jedenfalls   *in any event*
Jedenfalls sollten wir morgen noch mehr darüber sprechen.
In any event, we should talk more about that tomorrow.

jemals   *ever*
Warst du jemals in Berlin?
Have you ever been to Berlin?

jemand   *someone*
Ich suche jemanden, der den Kühlschrank reparieren kann.
I am looking for someone who can repair the refrigerator.

jenseits   *on the other side of*
Sie steht jenseits der Grenze und wartet auf ihn.
She is standing on the other side of the border and waiting for him.

jetzt   *now*
Jetzt ist es 17 Uhr.
It is now 5 p.m.

joggen   *to jog*
Er joggt gern durch die Stadt.
He likes to jog through the city.

Jom Kippur m.   *Yom Kippur*
Jom Kippur ist einer der wichtigsten Feiertage im Judentum.
Yom Kippur is one of the most important holidays in Judaism.

Judentum n.   *Judaism*
Das Judentum ist eine der wichtigsten Religionen der Welt.
Judaism is one of the most important religions in the world.

Jugend f.   *youth*
Die alte Dame vermisst ihre Jugend.
The old woman misses her youth.

Jugendliche(-n) m. and f.   *adolescent, teenager*
Die Jugendlichen spielen Fußball im Park.
The teenagers are playing soccer in the park.

Jugendstil m.   *art nouveau*
Der Jugendstil ist eine Kunstrichtung, die man an vielen Wiener
Fassaden bewundern kann.
*Art nouveau is an art form that you can admire on many Viennese
facades.*

jung   young
Wir sind nicht mehr jung.
We are no longer young.

Junge(-n) m.   *boy*
Der Junge singt mit dem anderen im Chor.
The boy is singing with the others in the choir.

K

Kabel n.   *cable*
Über ein Kabel verbindet man den Fernseher mit dem
DVD-Spieler.
You can connect the TV set to a DVD player with a cable.

Kabinett(-e) n.   *wardrobe*
Er legt die gefalteten Kleider ins Kabinett.
He puts the folded clothes into the wardrobe.

Kachel(-n) f.   *tile*
Er hat schöne Kacheln im Badezimmer installieren lassen.
He had pretty tiles installed in the bathroom.

Kachelofen(-öfen) m.   *tiled stove*
In Österreich heizen noch viele alte Häuser mit Kachelöfen.
In Austria, many older houses are still heated with a tiled stove.

Kaffeehaus(-häuser) n.   *café*
Viele Wiener sitzen gern im Kaffeehaus und lesen die Zeitung.
Many Viennese like to sit in a café and read the newspaper.

Kai(-s) m.   *quay*
Er spaziert mit seiner Freundin am Kai.
He goes for a walk with girlfriend along the quay.

Kaiser m.   *emperor*
Der Kaiser hat in der Hofburg in Wien gewohnt.
The emperor lived in Vienna's Hofburg.

Kaiserin(-nen) f.   *empress*
Kaiserin Maria-Theresia war eine wichtige Figur in der
Geschichte des 18. Jahrhunderts.
*Empress Maria Theresa was an important figure in the eighteenth
century.*

Kaktus(Kakteen) m.   *cactus*
Bastian hat sich an einem Kaktus gestochen.
Bastian pricked himself on a cactus.

Kalendar m.   *calendar*
Ich kann den Termin im Kalendar nicht finden.
I can't find the appointment on the calendar.

Kalifornien n.   *California*
Kalifornien ist ein Budesstaat an der Westküste der USA.
California is a state on the west coast of the U.S.A.

kalifornisch
Kalifornische Weine kann man jetzt auch in Deutschland
kaufen.
You can now buy Californian wines in Germany.

kalt   *cold*
Im Winter ist es in Mitteleuropa immer sehr kalt.
It is always very cold in Central Europe in winter.

Kälte f.   *cold*
Die Kälte war diesen Winter wirklich extreme.
The cold was really extreme this winter.

Kamera(-s) f.   *camera*
Er hat mehrere Fotos mit seiner Kamera gemacht.
He took several pictures with his camera.

Kamm(Kämme) m.   *comb*
Der Friseur braucht einen Kamm für seine Arbeit.
The hairdresser needs a comb for his work.

kämmen   *to comb*
Ursula kämmt sich die Haare.
Ursula combs her hair.

Kammer(-n) f.   *chamber*
Hinter der Küche befindet sich eine kleine Kammer für Vorräte.
Behind the kitchen there is a small chamber for supplies.

Kampf(Kämpfe) m.   *fight*
Er hat den Kampf gegen Krebs gewonnen.
He won the fight against cancer.

kämpfen   *to fight*
Sie kämpft für ihre Rechte.
She is fighting for her rights.

Kanada n.   *Canada*
Kanada ist das zweitgrößte Land der Welt.
Canada is the second largest country in the world.

Kanadier m. **Kanadierin(-nen)** f.   *Canadian person*
Herr Schwarz ist Kanadier und kommt aus Montreal.
Mr. Schwarz is a Canadian and comes from Montreal.

kanadisch   *Canadian*
Der kanadische Ahornsirup ist in der ganzen Welt bekannt.
Canadian maple syrup is famous throughout the whole world.

Kanal(Kanäle) m.   *canal*
In Venedig gibt es viele Kanäle.
The are many canals in Venice.

Kanton(-e) m.   *canton (Switzerland)*
Zürich ist einer von 23 Kantonen in der Schweiz.
Zurich is one of 23 cantons in Switzerland.

kaputt   *broken*
Der Fernseher ist kaputt, also müssen wir einen neuen kaufen.
The TV set is broken, so we will need to buy a new one.

Karte(-n) f.   *map*
Ich kann das Krankenhaus auf der Karte nicht finden.
I can't find the hospital on the map.

Katalog(-e) m.   *catalog*
Im Katalog stehen alle unsere Neuerscheinungen.
You will find all our new releases in our catalog.

kaufen   *to buy*
Herr und Frau Möller kaufen ein neues Haus.
Mr. and Mrs. Möller are buying a new house.

kaum   *barely*
Sie kennt den Bürgermeister kaum.
She barely knows the mayor.

Kaution(-en) f.   *deposit*
Er zahlt eine Kaution für den Kauf des Hauses.
He pays a deposit to buy the house.

Keller m.   *basement*
Im Keller steht die Waschküche.
The laundry room is in the basement.

kennen   *to know*
Er kennt alle seine Nachbarn
He knows all his neighbors.

kennen lernen   *to get to know*
Es freut mich, Sie kennen zu lernen.
It is nice to get to know you.

Kerl(-e) m.   *guy*
Rudi ist ein guter Kerl.
Rudi is a good guy.

Kerze(-n) f.   *candle*
Die Kerze ist über Nacht ausgebrannt.
The candle burned out overnight.

Kette(-n) f.   *necklace*
Sie hat eine goldene Kette zum Ball getragen.
She wore a golden necklace to the ball.

Kind(-er) n.   *child*
Das Kind geht gern in die Volksschule.
The child likes to go to elementary school.

Kindergarten(-gärten) m.   *pre-school, kindergarten*
Nicht alle Kinder in Deutschland gehen in den Kindergarten.
Not all children in Germany go to kindergarten.

Kinderzimmer n.   *children's room*
Die Kinder spielen im Kinderzimmer.
The children are playing in the children's room.

Kino(-s) n.   *movie theater*
Ich habe mir den neuen Film im Kino angesehen.
I watched the new film at the movie theater.

Kirche(-n) f.   *church*
Die Kirche befindet sich in der Mitte des Orts.
The church is located in the center of town.

Kissen n.   *pillow*
Er schläft gern auf einem weichen Kissen.
He likes to sleep on a soft pillow.

Kiste(-n) f.   *box*
Sie packt ihre Bücher in eine Kiste.
She is packing her books in a box.

Klage(-n) f.   *complaint*
Er hat eine Klage bei dem Gericht eingebracht.
He brought a complaint to court.

klagen   *to complain*
Er klagt über den Lärm der Nachbarn.
He complains about the neighbor's noise.

Klavier(-e) n.   *piano*
Elisabeth spielt eine Sonate auf dem Klavier.
Elisabeth is playing a sonata on the piano.

Klebeband(-bänder) n.   *tape*
Er klebt ein Foto an die Tür mit einem Klebeband.
He sticks a photo on the door with tape.

kleben   *to glue*
Er klebt die zwei Stücke Holz zusammen.
He glues the two pieces of wood together.

Klebstoff(-e) m.   *glue*
Er braucht Klebstoff, um etwas zu kleben.
He needs glue in order to glue something.

Kleiderbügel m.   *hanger*
Sie hängt das Hemd auf den Kleiderbügel.
She hangs the shirt on a hanger.

klein   *small*
Das kleine Haus steht zwischen zwei großen Häusern.
The small house sits between two large houses.

klettern   *to climb*
Der Junge klettert auf einen Baum.
The boy is climbing a tree.

Klima(-te) n.   *climate*
Das Klima in Mitteleuropa ist meistens mild.
The climate in Central Europe is mostly mild.

Klimaanlage(-n) f.   *air conditioning*
Im Sommer ist es angenehm, eine Klimaanlage in der Wohnung
zu haben.
*It is pleasant to have air conditioning in the apartment during the
summer.*

Klingel(-n) f.   *bell*
Er kann die Klingel nicht hören.
He can't hear the bell.

klingeln   *to ring*
Jemand klingelt an der Tür.
Someone is ringing the doorbell.

Klinik(-en) f.   *clinic*
Der Patient wird in der Klinik behandelt.
The patient is being treated at the clinic.

Klo(-s) n.   *toilet*
Das Klo befindet sich links von dem Badezimmer.
The toilet is located to the left of the bathroom.

Klopapier n.   *toilet paper*
Er kauft Klopapier im Supermarkt.
He buys toilet paper at the supermarket.

klopfen   *to knock*
Er klopft an die Tür.
He knocks on the door.

kneten   *knead*
Sie knetet den Brotteig für die Semmeln.
She is kneading the bread dough for the rolls.

Knopf(Knöpfe) m.   *button*
Diese Bluse hat acht Knöpfe.
This blouse has eight buttons.

Knoten m.   *knot*
Richard macht einen Knoten in das Seil, um auf den Baum zu
   klettern.
Richard ties a knot in the rope in order to climb up the tree.

kochen   *to cook*
Sie kocht eine schöne heiße Suppe.
She is cooking a nice hot soup.

Kochbuch(-bücher) n.   *cookbook*
In diesem Kochbuch findest du viele Rezepte zur ungarischen
   Küche.
You will find many Hungarian recipes in this cookbook.

Koffer m.   *suitcase*
Der Koffer ist erst mit Verspätung am Flughafen eingtroffen.
The suitcase was late in arriving at the airport.

Kombi(-s) m.   *station wagon*
Ein Kombi bietet mehr Platz als ein gewöhnlicher PKW.
A station wagon offers more room than a conventional car.

Kommode(-n) f.   *dresser*
Er legt die Hemden in die Kommode.
He puts the shirts into the dresser.

kompliziert   *complicated*
Das ist ein sehr kompliziertes Problem.
This is a very complicated problem.

komponieren   *to compose*
Beethoven hat seine neunte Symphonie komponiert.
Beethoven composed his ninth symphony.

Komposition(-en) f.   *composition*
Dieses Kunstwerk ist die beste Komposition des Künstlers.
This work of art is the artist's best composition.

Konferenz(-en) f.   *conference*
An der Konferenz haben Wissenschaftler aus mehreren Ländern
teilgenommen.
Scientists from several countries participated at the conference.

König(-e) m.   *king*
Johann Strauß ist in der Welt bekannt als der Walzerkönig.
Johann Strauss is known as "The Waltz King" throughout the world.

Königin(-nen) f.   *queen*
Die Königin der Niederlande hat den österreichischen
Bundespräsidenten besucht.
The Queen of the Netherlands visited the Austrian Federal President.

Königreich(-e) n.   *kingdom*
Bayern war bis 1918 ein Königreich.
Bavaria was a kingdom until 1918.

können   *to be able to*
Ich kann Deutsch sprechen.
I can speak German.

Konsument(-en) m. **Konsumentin(-nen)** f.   *consumer*
Konsumenten haben Rechte, die sie vor schlechten Verkäufern
schützen.
Consumers have rights that protect them from bad sellers.

Konto(-s) n.   *account*
Er behebt 100 Euro von seinem Konto.
He withdraws 100 euros from his account.

Konzert(-e) n.   *concert*
Ute und Uwe haben gestern das Konzert im Park genossen.
Ute and Uwe enjoyed the concert in the park yesterday.

Korb(Körbe) m.   *basket*
Maria legt die geernteten Marillen in den Korb.
Maria puts the harvested apricots into a basket.

Körper m.   *body*
Bruno trainiert viel, um seinen Körper fit zu halten.
Bruno works out a lot to keep his body fit.

kosten   *to cost*
Ein Kilo Äpfel kostet zwei Euro auf dem Markt.
A kilo of apples costs two euros at the market.

kostenlos   *free of charge*
Diese Broschüren sind kostenlos.
These brochures are free of charge.

Kraft(Kräfte) f.   *power*
Er hat nicht die Kraft, allein aufzustehen.
He does not have the power to stand alone.

kräftig   *strong*
Der kräftige junge Mann hilft uns beim Umzug.
The strong young man is helping us with the move.

krank   *sick*
Der kranke Mann geht zum Arzt.
The sick man goes to the doctor.

Krankenhaus(-häuser) n.   *hospital*
Sie liegt schon seit einer Woche im Krankenhaus.
She has been in the hospital for a week already.

Krankheit(-en) f.   *illness, disease*
Die Krankheit kann man behandeln, aber nicht heilen.
You can treat this illness, but not cure it.

Kraut(Kräuter) n.   *herb*
Sie kocht gern mit Kräutern.
She like to cook with herbs.

Kreditkarte(-n) f.   *credit card*
Hier können Sie mit Kreditkarte bezahlen.
You can pay here with a credit card.

Kreis(-e) m.   *circle*
Die Gruppe sitzt im Kreis.
The group is sitting in a circle.

kreisen   *to circle*
Das Flugzeug kreist vor der Landung über Frankfurt.
The airplane circles before landing in Frankfurt.

Kreislauf(-läufe) m.   *circulation*
Ein gesunder Kreislauf ist wichtig für das Herz.
A healthy circulation is important for the heart.

Kreuz(-e) m.   *cross*
In der Kirche hängen viele Kreuze.
Many crosses hang in the church.

Kreuzzug(-züge) m.   *crusade*
Die Kreuzzüge führten Europäer in den Nahen Osten.
The crusades led Europeans into the Middle East.

kriechen   *crawl*
Er kriecht unter den Tisch.
He crawls under the table.

Krieg(-e) m.   *war*
Er war Soldat im Krieg.
He was a soldier in the war.

Krimi(-s) m.   *murder mystery*
Sie liest gern schwedische Krimis.
She likes to read Swedish murder mysteries.

Krise(-n) f.   *crisis*
Die Regierung warnt vor einer tiefen Krise im Ausland.
The government warns about a serious crisis abroad.

Küche(-en) f.   *kitchen*
Er backt einen Kuchen in der Küche.
He is baking a cake in the kitchen.

Kugel(-n) f.   *ball*
Die Kinder spielen mit einer Kugel aus Glas.
The children are playing with a glass ball.

Kugelschreiber m.   *ballpoint pen*
Er unterschreibt seinen Namen mit einem Kugelschreiber.
He signs his name with a ballpoint pen.

kühl   *cool*
Im Herbst ist das Wetter in Deutschland kühl.
In fall, the weather is cool in Germany.

kühlen   *to chill*
Das Getränk muss gekühlt werden.
The drink needs to be chilled.

Kühlschrank(-schränke) m.   *refrigerator*
Die Milch findest du im Kühlschrank.
You will find the milk in the refrigerator.

Kultur(-en) f.   *culture*
Sie interessiert sich sehr für andere Kulturen.
She is very interested in other cultures.

Kummer m.   *grief*
Ich habe großen Kummer wegen der wirtschaftlichen Situation des Landes.
The economic situation of the country causes me a lot of grief.

kümmern   *to take care of*
Frau Gerstl kümmert sich um ihre ältere Nachbarin.
Ms. Gerstl takes care of her elderly neighbor.

Kunde(-n) m. **Kundin(-nen)** f.   *customer*
Der Kunde ist immer König.
The customer is always king.

Kundendienst(-e) m.   *customer service*
Herr Lang hat beim Kundendienst angerufen.
Mr. Lang called customer service.

Kunst(Künste) f.   *art*
Er interessiert sich für römische Kunst.
He is interested in Roman art.

Kunstgeschichte f.   *art history*
Hilde studiert Kunstgeschichte an der Universität Wien.
Hilde is studying art history at the University of Vienna.

Kunststoff(-e) m.   *plastic*
Das Material für die Möbel ist aus Kunststoff.
The material for the furniture is made of plastic.

Kunststück(-e) n.   *piece/work of art*
Der Sprung des Schispringers ist ein Kunststück.
The leap of the ski jumper is a work of art.

Kunstwerk(-e) n.   *work of art*
In diesem Museum findet man viele Kunstwerke.
You can find many works of art in this museum.

Kupfer n.   *copper*
Diese Münze ist aus Kupfer.
This coin is made of copper.

Kurs(-e) m.   *course*
Arkan belegt einen Kochkurs.
Arkan is taking a cooking course.

kurz   *short*
Die Ärmel auf diesem Hemd sind zu kurz.
The sleeves on this shirt are too short.

Kürze f.   *short(ness)*
Die Kürze der Ansprache ist beim Publikum gut angekommen.
The shortness of the speech was welcomed by the audience.

kuscheln   *to cuddle*
Das Paar kuschelt beim Feuer.
The couple cuddles by the fire.

Kuss(Küsse) m.   *kiss*
Er gibt ihr einen Kuss auf die Wange.
He gives her a kiss on the cheek.

küssen   *to kiss*
Sie küssen sich zum Abschied.
They kiss each other goodbye.

Küste(-n) f.   *coast*
Lübeck ist eine Stadt an der Ostseeküste.
Lübeck is a city on the Baltic Sea coast.

L

Labor(-e) n.   *laboratory*
Das Blut wird im Labor untersucht.
The blood is being tested in the lab.

lächeln   *to smile*
Die Verkäuferin lächelt zu ihren Kunden
The salesperson smiles at her customers.

lachen   *to laugh*
Als ich den Witz gehört habe, musste ich ganz einfach lachen.
When I heard the joke, I just had to laugh.

Lack m.   *paint*
Der Lack auf dem Auto schaut nicht mehr gut aus.
The paint on the car doesn't look good anymore.

Lade(-n) f.   *drawer*
Das Besteck ist in der Lade.
The cutlery is in the drawer.

laden   *to load*
Ich lade eine Batterie in die Fernbedienung.
I load a battery into the remote control.

Ladung(-en) f.   *load*
Der LKW hat eine Ladung Holz von Kroatien nach Dänemark befördert.
The truck transported a load of wood from Croatia to Denmark.

Lager n.   *camp*
Im Sommer schlagen die Pfadfinder hier ihr Lager auf.
The boy scouts put up their camp here in summer.

Lampe(-n) f.   *lamp*
Mach bitte die Lampe an, damit wir hier mehr Licht haben.
Please turn on the lamp so we have more light.

Land(Länder) n.   *country*
Deutsch wird in mehreren Ländern Europas gesprochen.
German is spoken in several European countries.

Landebahn(-en) f.   *runway*
Der Flughafen in Wien hat zwei Landebahnen.
The airport in Vienna has two runways.

landen   *to land*
Das Flugzeug ist schon in Warschau gelandet.
The airplane already landed in Warsaw.

Landstraße(-n) f.   *country road*
Wenn auf der Landstraße fährt, sieht man mehr als von der Autobahn.
You will see more if you drive on a country road rather than on the highway.

lang   *long*
Sie trägt ein langes Kleid zum Ball.
She is wearing a long dress to the ball.

Länge(-e) f.   *length*
Die Länge der Hose passt ja wunderbar.
The pant length fits great.

langsam   *slow*
Fahren Sie bitte etwas langsamer.
Please drive a litte bit slower.

langweilig   *boring*
Das war ein langweiliger Film, der mich nicht gefallen hat.
That was a boring film that I did not like.

Last(-en) f.   *burden*
Dieser Gast ist eine große Last für die Familie.
This guest is a great burden on the family.

lästig   *annoying*
Der Lärm der Nachbarn ist einfach sehr lästig.
The neighbors' noise is just very annoying.

Lätzchen n.   *bib*
Die Mutter wäscht das Lätzchen ihres Babys.
The mother washes her baby's bib.

Lauf(Läufe) m.   *run, course*
Manchmal wiederholt sich der Lauf der Geschichte.
Sometimes the course of history repeats itself.

laufen   *to run*
Die Kinder laufen um den Park.
The children run around the park.

Laune(-n) f.   *mood*
Er is heute so nett, weil er gute Laune hat.
He is so nice today because he is in a good mood.

launisch   *moody*
Der Vater hat gestern einen schlechten Tag gehabt und ist
    launisch heute.
The father had a bad day yesterday and is moody today.

laut   *loud*
Sie hört gern laute Musik.
She likes to listen to loud music.

Lautstärke f.   *volume*
Die Lautstärke muss auf diesem Radio eingestellt werden.
The volume needs to be adjusted on this radio.

Leben n.   *life*
Er hat ein langes, glückliches Leben gelebt.
He lives a long happy life.

leben   *to live*
Die Familie lebt in einem Haus in Klagenfurt.
The family lives in a house in Klagenfurt.

lecken   *to lick*
Das Kind leckt entzückt am Eis.
The child excitedly licks the ice cream.

lecker   *tasty*
Das ist ein leckerer Kuchen.
This is a tasty cake.

Leder n.   *leather*
Die Schuhe sind aus gutem Leder.
The shoes are made of good leather.

lehren   *to teach*
Der Professor lehrt an der Universität.
The professor teaches at the university.

Leiche(-n) f.   *corpse*
Ein toter Körper ist eine Leiche.
A dead body is a corpse.

leicht   *light*
Das ist ein leichter Koffer, denn ich ohne Mühe tragen kann.
This is a light suitcase that I can carry without trouble.

Leid(-en) n.   *suffering*
Das Leid der Überlebenden der Katastrophe is unfassbar.
The suffering of the survivors of the catastrophe is incomprehensible.

leider   *unfortunately*
Leider konnten wir nicht länger Urlaub machen.
Unfortunately, we couldn't stay on vacation any longer.

Leine(-n) f.   *leash*
Im Park müssen die Hunde an der Leine geführt werden.
Dogs have to be kept on a leash in the park.

leise   *quiet*
Er geht leise durch die Wohnung, weil er seine Familie nicht
    aufwecken will.
*He moves quietly through the apartment because he does not want
    to wake his family.*

leisten   *to afford*
Sie kann sich eine schöne große Wohnung im 1. Bezirk Wiens
    leisten.
She can afford a nice big apartment in the first district of Vienna.

Leistung(-en) f.   *achievement*
Das war eine tolle Leistung des Sportlers.
This was a great achievement for the athlete.

Leiter(-n) f.   *ladder*
Ich brauche eine Leiter, um auf das Dach zu klettern.
I need a ladder to climb onto the roof.

lenken   *to drive*
Der Chauffeur lenkt einen großen Kombi.
The driver is driving a large station wagon.

Lenkrad(-räder) n.   *steering wheel*
Der Fahrer halt das Lenkrad fest.
The driver holds on tight to the steering wheel.

lernen   *to learn, to study*
Die Studenten lernen Deutsch.
The students are studying German.

Leute pl.   *people*
In der Innenstadt habe ich viele Leute gesehen.
I saw many people downtown.

Lexikon(-a) n.   *encyclopedia*
Dieses Konzept habe ich im Lexikon nachgeschlagen.
I looked up the concept in the encyclopedia.

Licht(-er) n.   *light*
Wenn er schlafen geht, dreht er das Licht ab.
He turns off the light when he goes to bed.

lieb   *dear, cute*
Dieses kleine Kind ist so lieb.
This small child is so cute.

Liebe(-n) f.   *love*
Die Liebe ist wichtiger als das Geld.
Love is more important than money.

lieben   *to love*
Die Kinder lieben Zeichentrickfilme im Fernsehen.
The cildren love TV cartoons.

Liechtenstein n.   *Liechtenstein*
Liechtenstein befindet sich zwischen Österreich und der Schweiz.
Liechtenstein is located between Austria and Switzerland

Lied(-er) n.   *song*
Die Mutter singt ihrem Sohn ein Lied vor.
The mother is singing a song for her son.

Literatur(-en) f.   *literature*
Malvine liest gern die Klassiker der russischen Literatur.
Malvine likes to read the classics of Russian literature.

LKW(-s) m.   *truck*
Der LKW fährt auf der Autobahn.
The truck is driving on the highway.

Lob(-e) n.   *praise*
Für seine Arbeit hat sehr viel Lob bekommen.
He got lots of praise for his work.

loben   *to praise*
Die Lehrerin lobt die Arbeit ihrer Schüler.
The teacher praises the work of her students.

Loch(Löcher) n.   *hole*
Er hat ein Loch in seinen Socken gefunden.
He found a hole in his socks.

Löffel(-n) m.   *spoon*
Suppe isst man mit dem Löffel.
You eat soup with a spoon.

Lohn(Löhne) m.   *salary*
Die Demonstranten fordern gleiche Löhne für Männer und Frauen.
The demonstrators demand equal salaries for men and women.

los   *go*
Achtung, fertig, los!
Get ready, get set, go!

Lösung(-en) f.   *solution*
Wir suchen nach einer Lösung des Problems.
We are searching for a solution to the problem.

Lotterie(-n) f.   *lottery*
Sie spielt gern in der Lotterie.
She likes to play the lottery.

Luft(Lüfte) f.   *air*
In den Alpen ist die Qualität der Luft immer ausgezeichnet.
The air quality is always excellent in the Alps.

Luftballon(-e) m.   *balloon*
Die Kinder haben im Vergnügungspark Luftballone bekommen.
The children got balloons at the amusement park.

Lupe(-n) f.   *magnifying glass*
Er untersucht seine Briefmarkensammlung mit einer Lupe.
He examines his stamp collection with a magnifying glass.

lustig   *funny*
Sie hat mir eine lustige Geschichte erzählt.
She told me a funny story.

Luxemburg n.   *Luxembourg*
Luxemburg ist ein Land, in dem man Französisch und Deutsch
    spricht.
Luxembourg is a country where people speak French and German.

M

machbar   *feasible*
Diese Pläne sind durchaus machbar.
These plans are completely feasible.

machen   *to do*
Was macht ihr gern im Urlaub?
What do you all like to do on vacation?

Mädchen n.   *girl*
Die Mädchen spielen nach der Schule Volleyball.
The girls play volleyball after school.

Magnet(-e) m.   *magnet*
Auf ihrem Kühlschrank hat sie mehrere Magneten.
She has several magnets on her refrigerator.

mähen   *to mow*
Yagmur mäht das Gras hinter ihrem Haus
Yagmur is mowing the lawn behind her house.

Mahlzeit(-en) f.   *meal*
Im Gasthause bereiten sie eine festliche Mahlzeit vor.
They are preparing a festive meal at the inn.

mal   *times*
Diese Woche musste ich fünf mal zum Arzt laufen.
This week I had to go to the doctor five times.

Malbuch(-bücher) n.   *coloring book*
Die Kinder malen in ihre Malbücher.
The children color in their coloring books.

malen *to paint*
Er malt gern Bilder von der bayrischen Landschaft.
He likes to paint pictures of the Bavarian landscape.

Malerei(-en) f. *painting*
In der Gallerie wurden schöne Malereien von Klimt gezeigt.
The gallery displayed beautiful paintings by Klimt.

malerisch *picturesque*
Uns gefällt die malerischen Landschaften in der Schweiz.
We like the picturesque landscapes in Switzerland

manchmal *sometimes*
Manchmal gehen wir am Nachmittag ins Kaffeehaus.
Sometimes we go to the café in the afternoon.

Mangel(Mängel) m. *lack*
Er leidet unter einem Mangel an Verständnis für seine Frau.
He suffers from a lack of understanding of his wife.

Manieren pl. *manners*
Die Kinder haben gute Manieren und sagen immer schön bitte und danke.
The children have good manners and always politely say please and thank you.

Mann(Männer) m. *man*
Der Mann sitzt im Gasthaus neben seiner Frau.
The man is sitting next to his wife at the inn.

Mannschaft(-en) f. *team*
Die Mannschaft hat das Spiel in Aachen gewonnen.
The team won the game in Aachen.

Mappe(-n) f. *folder*
In Ihrer Mappe finden Sie weitere Informationen zu unserer Firma.
In your folder you will find further information on our company.

Märchen n. *fairy tale*
Die Gebrüder Grimm haben viele Märchen aufgeschrieben.
The Brothers Grimm wrote down many fairy tales.

Markt(Märkte) m. *market*
Jeden Samstag gibt es im Dorf einen Markt.
There is a market in the village every Saturday.

Maschine(-n) f.   *machine*
Herr Lange wartet die Maschine.
Mr. Lange maintains the machine.

Masse(-n) f.   *mass, majority*
Die Masse der Bevölkerung unterstützt den Präsidenten.
The majority of the population supports the president.

Matratze(-n) f.   *mattress*
Die Matratze liegt auf dem Bett.
The mattress is lying on the bed.

Matura f.   *high school final exam (in Austria and Switzerland)*
Ohne Matura kann man in Österreich und der Schweiz nicht
  studieren.
*You can't study at a university in Austria and Switzerland without
  passing the high school final exam.*

Mauer(-n) f.   *wall*
Reste der Berliner Mauer kann man auch heute noch besichtigen.
You can still see remainders of the Berlin Wall to this day.

Maut(-en) f.   *toll*
Auf den Autobahnen in Österreich und der Schweiz muss man
  eine Maut bezahlen.
You have to pay a toll on the highways in Austria and Switzerland.

Medizin f.   *medicine*
Für diese Krankheit gibt es keine Medizin.
There is no medicine for this illness.

Meer(-e) n.   *ocean*
Das Schiff fährt über das Meer.
The ship crosses the ocean.

mehr   *more*
Ich hätte gern mehr Suppe, bitte.
I would like more soup, please.

Mehrheit(-en) f.   *majority*
Die Mehrheit der Wähler hat für die Partei des Kanzlers
  gestimmt.
The majority of the voters voted for the chancellor's party.

Meldeamt(-ämter) n.   *residence registration office*
Am Meldeamt müssen sich alle Bewohner melden.
All residents need to be registered at the residence registration office.

melden   *to report*
Frau Schatzinger meldet den Vorfall der Polizei.
Ms. Schatzinger reports the incident to the police.

Meldezettel m.   *residence registration card*
Wenn Sie in Österreich wohnen wollen, brauchen Sie einen
   Meldezettel.
If you want to live in Austria, you need a residence registration card.

Menge(-n) f.   *crowd*
Die Mutter hat ihren Sohn in der Menge fast verloren.
The mother almost lost her son in the crowd.

Mensa(-Mensen) f.   *university cafeteria*
Die Studenten essen in der Mensa.
The students are eating at the university cafeteria.

Mensch(-en) m.   *person, people*
Herr Kowar ist ein guter Mensch.
Mr. Kowar is a good person.

menschlich   *human*
Irren ist menschlich.
To err is human.

merken   *to memorize*
Sie merkt sich die Handynummer ihres Freundes.
She memorizes her boyfriend's cell phone number.

Messe(-n) f.   *fair, convention*
Auf der Messe wurden viele neue Produkte angeboten.
Many new products were displayed at the fair.

messen   *to measure*
Er misst die Größe des Zimmers.
He measures the size of the room.

Messer n.   *knife*
Er schneidet sich mit dem Messer ein Stück von der Wurst.
He cuts a slice of sausage with the knife.

Miete(-n) f.   *rent*
Die Miete für die Wohnung beträgt 625 Euro kalt pro Monat.
The rent for the apartment is 625 euros per month without utilities.

mieten   *to rent*
Er mietet sich ein Auto am Flughafen in Bremen.
He rents a car at the airport in Bremen.

Mikrowellenherd(-e) f.   *microwave oven*
Der Mikrowellenherd steht neben dem Kühlschrank.
The microwave is next to the fridge.

mild   *mild*
In der mexikanischen Küche habe ich lieber die milden Saucen.
I prefer the mild salsas of Mexican cusine.

Milieu(-s) n.   *environment*
Mir gefällt das Milieu dieser Stadt nicht.
I do not like this city's environment.

Minderheit(-en) f.   *minority*
Im deutschen Bundesland Schleswig-Holstein gibt es eine
   dänische Minderheit.
There is a Danish minority in the German state of Schleswig-
   Holstein.

mindestens   *at least*
Wir brauchen mindestens 500 Euro, um die Reise zu
   finanzieren.
We need at least 500 euros to fund the trip.

Müll m.   *trash*
Der Müll wird jeden Donnerstag hier abgeholt.
The trash is picked up here every Thursday.

Mülleimer m.   *trash can*
Sie wirft die Verpackungen in den Mülleimer.
She throws the packagings into the trash can.

mit   *with*
Ich hätte gern ein Paar Frankfurter mit Senf.
I would like a couple of hot dogs with mustard.

mitarbeiten   *to collaborate*
Wenn Sie wollen, können Sie gern an diesem Projekt
   mitarbeiten.
If you like, you are welcome to collaborate on this project.

Mitarbeiter m. **Mitarbeiterin(-nen)** f.   *co-worker, employee*
Unsere Firma hat über 50 Mitarbeiter.
Our company has more than 50 employees.

mitbringen   *to bring along/with*
Aus ihrem Urlaub haben sie uns ein Andenken mitgebracht.
They brought us a souvenir from their vacation.

Mitglied(-er) n.   *member*
Sie ist Mitglied im Sportverein.
She is a member of the sports club.

mitkommen   *to come along/with*
Franz kommt mit uns nach Venedig mit.
Franz is coming with us to Venice.

mitmachen   *to participate*
Sie will bei unserer Demonstration mitmachen.
She wants to participate in our demonstration.

mitnehmen   *to take along*
Wir nehmen einen Imbiss auf die Wanderung mit.
We are taking a snack along on our hike.

Mitte(-n) f.   *middle*
In der Mitte des Zimmers befindet sich ein Tisch.
In the middle of the room there is a table.

mitteilen   *to communicate*
Man hat mir soeben die Nachricht mitgeteilt.
The message was just communicated to me.

Mitteilung(-en) f.   *message*
Er hat eine wichtige Mitteilung von seinem Chef bekommen.
He received an important message from his boss.

Mittel n.   *means*
Ich habe nicht genügend Mittel, das Haus zu renovieren.
I do not have enough means to renovate the house.

Mitteleuropa n.   *Central Europe*
Deutschland und Österreich sind Länder in Mitteleuropa.
Germany and Austria are countries in Central Europe.

Mittelmeer n.   *Mediterranean Sea*
Im Sommer fahren viele Deutsche gern ans Mittelmeer.
In summer, many Germans like to travel to the Mediterranean Sea.

mittlerweile   *in the meantime*
Mittlerweile haben wir unsere Meinung geändert.
In the meantime, we changed our mind.

Möbel f.   *furniture*
Sie hat sehr alte Möbel in ihrer Wohnung.
She has very old furniture in her apartment.

Mode(-n) f.   *fashion*
Steffi interessiert sich sehr für Mode und liest immer
  Modezeitschriften.
*Steffi is very interested in fashion and is always reading fashion
  magazines.*

modisch   *fashionable*
Sie fährt gern nach Paris, um modische Kleider in den Boutiquen
  zu kaufen.
She likes to go to Paris to buy fashionable clothes in the boutiques.

mögen   *to like*
Er mag Salzburg.
He likes Salzburg.

möglich   *possible*
Alles ist möglich, aber nichts ist gewiss.
Anything is possible, but nothing is certain.

Monarchie(-n) f.   *monarchy*
Österreich-Ungarn war eine Monarchie in Mitteleuropa.
Austria-Hungary was a monarchy in Central Europe.

Monat(-e) m.   *month*
Januar ist der erste Monat im Jahr.
January is the first month of the year.

Mond(-e) m.   *moon*
In der Nacht gibt der Mond ein blaues Licht ab.
At night the moon shines blue.

Mord(-e) m.   *murder*
Der Mord ist von der Polizei untersucht worden.
The murder was investigated by the police.

Mörder m. **Mörderin(-nen)** f.   *murderer*
Der Mörder ist zu lebenlanger Haft verurteilt worden.
The murderer was sentenced to life in prison.

Morgen m.   *morning*
Am Morgen zwitschern die Vögel immer so schön.
In the morning the birds always chirp so nicely.

morgen   *tomorrow*
Morgen fährt er auf eine Konferenz nach Brüssel.
He is traveling to a conference in Brussels tomorrow.

Moschee(-n) f.   *mosque*
In einer Moschee beten Menschen moslemischen Glaubens.
People of the Muslim faith pray in a mosque.

Motor(-en) m.   *motor*
Er ruft den ADAC, weil der Motor nicht anspringt und der
   Wagen abgeschleppt werden muss.
He calls AAA because the motor won't start and the car needs to be towed.

Mühe(-n) f.   *trouble*
Vielen Dank für all Ihre Mühle!
Thanks so much for all your trouble!

Mühle(-n) f.   *mill*
In der Mühle wird das Mehl gemahlen.
Flour is ground at the mill.

mündlich   *oral*
An deutschen Universitäten gibt es oft mündliche Prüfungen.
German universities often have oral exams.

Mundspülung(-en) f.   *mouth wash*
Nach dem Zähneputzen verwendet er eine Mundspülung.
After brushing his teeth, he uses mouth wash.

Münze(-n) f.   *coin*
Ich brauche eine Münze, um die Parkgebühr zu bezahlen.
I need a coin to pay the parking fee.

Museum(Museen) n.   *museum*
Im Museum gibt es derzeit eine interessante Ausstellung zur
   Biedermeier Kunst.
*There is currently an interesting exhibition on Biedermeier art at
   the museum.*

Musik f.   *music*
Hans hört Musik auf seinem iPhone.
Hans is listening to music on his iPhone.

musizieren   *to make music*
Die Kinder musizieren in der Schule.
The children are making music at school.

müssen   *to have to*
Ich muss zur Bank.
I have to go to the bank.

Muster n.   *sample*
Dieses Kleid können Sie nicht kaufen, denn es ist nur ein Muster.
You can't buy this dress because it is only a sample.

N

nach   *to, after*
Raingard fährt mit ihrem Mann nach Bad Ischl.
Raingard is driving to Bad Ischl with her husband.

Nachbar(-n) m. **Nachbarin(-nen)** f.   *neighbor*
Unsere Nachbarin kümmert sich um unsere Katze, wenn wir
auf Urlaub sind.
Our neighbor takes care of our cat when we are on vacation.

Nachbarschaft(-en) f.   *neighborhood*
In dieser Nachbarschaft gibt es viele kleine Geschäfte.
There are many small stores in this neighborhood.

nachdenken   *to think about*
Ich muss über den Vertrag noch nachdenken.
I still have to think about the contract.

Nachricht(-en) f.   *message, news*
Ich habe sofort die guten Nachrichten bekommen.
I immediately got the good news.

nachschauen   *to check*
Ich muss nachschauen, wann mein Reisepass abläuft.
I have to check when my passport expires.

nachschlagen   *to look up*
Er schlägt ein Wort im Wörterbuch nach.
He looks up a word in the dictionary.

Nacht(Nächte) f.   *night*
Sie hat die ganze Nacht für die Prüfung gelernt.
She studied all night for the exam.

Nachtisch(-e) m.   *dessert*
Zum Nachtisch habe ich einen Apfelstrudel bestellt.
I ordered apple strudel for dessert.

Nachtkasten(-kästen) m.   *night stand*
Auf ihrem Nachtkasten steht der Wecker.
The alarm clock is on her night stand.

Nadel(-n) f.   *needle*
Sie näht mit einer Nadel.
She is sewing with a needle.

Nagel(Nägel) m.   *nail*
Er hat zwei Nägel in das Brett eingeschlagen.
He nailed two nails into the board.

Nagellack(-e) m.   *nail polish*
Nagellack kann man in der Drogerie in verschiedenen Farben
  kaufen.
You can buy nail polish in various colors at the drugstore.

nah   *closeby*
Das Rathaus ist nah.
City hall is closeby.

nähen   *to sew*
Sie näht ein Kleid für ihre Freundin.
She is sewing a dress for her friend.

nass   *wet*
Plötzlich hat es zu regnen begonnen und wir sind nass geworden.
Suddenly it started to rain and we got wet.

Nazizeit f.   *Nazi era*
In der Nazizeit haben die Deutschen viele Verbrechen gegen die
  Menschheit begangen.
*During the Nazi era, the Germans committed many crimes against
  humanity.*

Nebel m.   *fog*
An der Nordseeküste gibt es im Winter oft viel Nebel
There is often a lot of fog on the North Sea coast in winter.

nebelig   *foggy*
Wenn es sehr nebelig ist, muss der Flughafen gesperrt werden.
When it is very foggy, the airport has to be closed.

neben   *next to*
Die Spülmaschine steht neben dem Kühlschrank.
The dishwasher is next to the refrigerator.

nebenan   *next door*
Die Wicherts wohnen nebenan.
The Wicherts live next door.

nehmen *to take*
Wir nehmen zwei Koffer auf die Reise.
We are taking two suitcases on our trip.

nein *no*
Nein, so machen wir das nicht!
No, we will not do it that way!

nervös *nervous*
Der Student ist wegen der Prüfung nervös.
The student is nervous because of the exam.

nett *nice, friendly*
Julia ist so nett, denn sie grüßt uns immer, wenn sie uns sieht.
Julia is so nice because she always says hello when she sees us.

neu *new*
Stefan kauft sich ein neues Auto.
Stefan is buying a new car.

nieder *low, primitive*
Er hat einen niederen Geschmack.
He has a primitive sense of taste.

Niederlande pl. *Netherlands*
Anne Frank wohnte während des Holocausts in den
Niederlanden.
Anne Frank lived in the Netherlands during the Holocaust.

niederländisch *Dutch*
Sie isst gern niederländischen Käse.
She likes to eat Dutch cheese.

niesen *to sneeze*
Er hat einen Schnupfen und muss oft niesen.
He has a cold and has to sneeze often.

nicht *not*
Das Kind will nicht schlafen gehen.
The child does not want to go to sleep.

nichts *nothing*
Wir haben nichts zu essen.
We have nothing to eat.

nicken *to nod*
Der Mann nickt seiner Frau zu.
The man nods to his wife.

nie   *never*
Er war noch nie auf Hawaii.
He has never been to Hawaii.

niemand   *nobody*
Es ist niemand zur Veranstaltung gekommen.
Nobody came to the event.

nirgendwann   *at no time, never*
Das wird nirgendwann passieren.
That will never happen.

nirgendwas   *nothing at all*
Ich brauche nirgendwas.
I need nothing at all.

nirgendwo   *nowhere*
Nirgendwo habe ich eine bessere Sachertorte gegessen als in Wien.
Nowhere did I eat a better Sacher torte than in Vienna.

Niveau(-s) n.   *level*
Die Studenten haben schon ein hohes Niveau erreicht.
The students have already reached a high level.

Norden m.   *north*
Schleswig-Holstein liegt im Norden von Deutschland.
Schleswig-Holstein is located in the north of Germany.

Nordsee f.   *North Sea*
Die Nordsee liegt zwischen Deutschland und England.
The North Sea is located between Germany and England.

Not(Nöte) f.   distress
Die Nachbarn helfen der Familie in Not.
The neighbors help the family in distress.

Notfall(-fälle) m.   *emergency*
Im Notfall rufen Sie bitte diese Nummer.
In case of an emergency, please call this number.

nötig   *necessary, required*
Haben Sie die nötigen Dokumente mitgebracht?
Did you bring the required documents along?

Notiz(-en) f.   *note*
In der Vorlesung habe ich keine Notizen gemacht.
I did not take notes during the lecture.

Notizblock(-blöcke) m.   *notebook*
Er schreibt die Information in seinen Notizblock.
He writes the information in his notebook.

notwendig   *necessary*
Haben Sie das notwendige Geld dieses Auto zu kaufen?
Do you have the necessary money to buy this car?

nun   *now*
Nun fahren wir nach Hause.
Now we are going home.

Nutzen m.   *use*
Die Maschine hat keinen Nutzen.
This machine is of no use.

nützlich   *useful*
Marienkäfer sind nützliche Tiere, weil sie andere Insekten
   essen.
Ladybugs are useful animals because they eat other insects.

O

oben   *up there*
Oben auf dem Berg hat er eine Hütte.
He has a cabin up on the mountain.

obwohl   *although*
Obwohl es heute regnet, gehen wir alle spazieren.
Although it is raining today, we are all going for a walk.

O-Bus(-se) m.   *trolleybus*
Mit dem O-Bus kann man ganz Salzburg erkunden.
You can explore all of Salzburg by trolleybus.

oder   *or*
Möchtest du das Salz oder den Pfeffer?
Would you like salt or pepper?

offen   *open*
Kommen Sie bitte herein, die Tür ist offen.
Please come in, the door is open.

offenbar   *apparently*
Offenbar ist das Konzert schon ausverkauft.
Apparently the concert is already sold out.

Öffentlichkeit(-en) f.   *public*
Er geht mit den Nachrichten an die Öffentlichkeit.
He is taking his news to the public.

offiziell   *official*
Sie hat eine offizielle Einladung zum Empfang erhalten.
She received an official invitation to the reception.

öffnen   *to open*
Kannst du mir bitte helfen, die Dose zu öffnen?
Can you please help me open the can?

ohne   *without*
Ohne Regenschirm geht Inge bei Schlechtwetter nicht aus dem
    Haus.
Inge does not leave the house in bad weather without an umbrella.

Ohnmacht f.   *helplessness*
Angesichts des Unglücks hat die Familie das Gefühl der
    Ohnmacht befallen.
The family felt a sense of helplessness when faced with misfortune

ohnmächtig   *powerless*
In dieser Situation fühlt sich der gewöhnliche Bürger ohnmächtig
    gegenüber den Behörden.
In this situation, the average citizen feels powerless against the authorities.

Öl(-e) n.   *oil*
Das Öl muss bei diesem Wagen gewechselt werden.
The oil needs to be changed in this car.

Oper(-n) f.   *opera*
Karl und seine Frau gehen am Samstagabend in die Oper.
Karl and his wife are going to the opera on Saturday evening.

Operation(-en) f.   *surgery*
Wolfgang hat die schwere Operation gut überstanden.
Wolfgang went through major surgery well.

Operette(-n) f.   *operetta*
In Wien wurden viele Operetten komponiert.
Many operettas were composed in Vienna.

Opfer n.   *victim*
Unser Nachbar hat die Nazizeit überlebt und ist Opfer des
    Faschismus.
Our neighbor survived the Nazi era and is a victim of Fascism.

Opferung(-en) f.   *sacrifice*
Im Alten Testament findet man Opferungen von Lämmern.
The Old Testament contains sacrifices of lambs.

Orchester n.   *orchestra*
Das Orchester spielt ein Konzert in Basel.
The orchestra is playing a concert in Basel.

ordentlich   *proper*
Er macht seine Arbeit immer ordentlich und niemand hat sich
    über ihn beschwert.
He always does his job properly and nobody has complained about him.

ordinär   *vulgar*
Ordinäre Ausdrücke sollten vor Kindern vermieden werden.
Vulgar expressions should be avoided in front of children.

Ordnung(-en) f.   *order*
Die Polizei sieht nach Recht und Ordnung.
The police look after law and order.

Organisation(-en) f.   *organization*
Diese Organisation hilft bedürftigen Menschen.
This organization helps people in need.

Organismus(Organismen) m.   *organism*
Im Meer befinden sich viele lebende Organismen.
Many living organisms can be found in the ocean.

Orientierung(-en) f.   *orientation*
Zur Orientierung gebe ich Ihnen jetzt eine Karte.
I will give you a map so you can find your orientation.

Original(-e) n.   *original*
Dieses Buch ist das Original in der Serie.
This book is the original one in the series.

Orkan(-e) m.   *hurricane*
Der Orkan hat zahlreiche Dächer von den Häusern geweht.
The hurricane blew numerous roofs off of houses.

Ort(-e) m.   *place*
In diesem Ort finde ich kein anständiges Kaffeehaus.
I can't find a decent café in this place.

Osten m.   *east*
Die Ukraine liegt im Osten Europas.
Ukraine is located in Eastern Europe.

Ostern n.   *Easter*
Ostern ist ein wichtiger Feiertag im Christentum.
Easter is an important holiday in Christianity.

Österreich n.   *Austria*
Österreich ist ein deutschsprachiges Land in Mitteleuropa.
Austria is a German-speaking country in Central Europe.

Österreicher m. **Österreicherin(-nen)** f.   *Austrian person*
Herr Aichinger ist Österreicher und kommt aus Bregenz.
Mr. Aichinger is Austrian and comes from Bregenz.

österreichisch   *Austrian*
Robert interessiert sich sehr für die österreichische Literatur.
Robert is really interested in Austrian literature.

Ostsee f.   *Baltic See*
Das deutsche Bundesland Mecklenburg-Vorpommern liegt an der Ostsee.
The German state of Mecklenburg-Vorpommern borders the Baltic Sea.

P

Paar(-e) n.   *pair, couple*
Er kauft sich ein Paar Schuhe im Einkaufszentrum.
He is buying a pair of shoes at the mall.

paar   *a few*
Er kauft sich ein paar Hemden im Einkaufszentrum.
He is buying a few shirts at the mall.

Paket(-e) n.   *package*
In der Post habe ich ein großes Paket bekommen.
I got a big package in the mail.

Palast(Paläste) m.   *palace*
Im Palast der Republik in Berlin war das Parlament der DDR.
The GDR parliament met in the Palace of the Republic in Berlin.

Palme(-n) f.   *palm tree*
Walter liegt gern unter Palmen am Strand.
Walter likes to lie beneath the palm trees on the beach.

Papier(-e) n.   *paper*
Wir schreiben unsere Arbeiten auf Papier.
We are completing our exam on paper.

Papiertuch(-tücher) n.   *paper towel*
Die Papiertücher hängen an der Wand in der Küche.
The paper towels are hanging on the wall in the kitchen.

Parfüm(-e) n.   *perfume*
Helga hat sich in der Parfümerie ein neues Parfüm gekauft.
Helga bought a new perfume at the perfume store.

Park(-s) m.   *park*
An einem sonnigen Tag ist es schön, im Park spazieren zu gehen.
It is nice to go for a walk in the park on a sunny day.

parken   *to park*
Frau Schmidt parkt ihr Auto in der Garage.
Ms. Schmidt is parking her car in the garage.

Parkett n.   *wooden floor*
Die Paare tanzen fröhlich auf dem Parkett.
The couples are dancing happily on the wooden floor.

Partei(-n) f.   *(political) party*
In Deutschland gibt es mehrere wichtige Parteien.
There are several important political parties in Germany.

Party(-s) f.   *party*
Gehst du morgen auf Herberts Party?
Are you going to Herbert's party tomorrow?

Passagier(-e) m.   *passanger*
In diesem Flugzeug haben über 200 Passagiere Platz.
More than 200 passangers can fit in this airplane.

passieren   *to happen*
In der letzten Folge der Seifenoper ist viel passiert.
A lot happened on the last episode of the soap opera.

pauken   *to cram*
Für die morgige Prüfung müssen wir noch ordentlich pauken.
We really need to cram for tomorrow's exam.

Pause(-n) f.   *break*
In einer Stunde machen wir eine kleine Pause von der Arbeit
     und trinken Kaffee.
In an hour we will take a short break from work and drink coffee.

Pech n.   *bad luck*
Er hatte wieder einmal Pech, denn er hat seine Stelle verloren.
He had bad luck again because he lost his job.

peinlich   *embarrassing*
Rudi findet es peinleich, wenn seine Mutter laut lacht.
Rudi thinks it is embarrassing when his mother laughs loudly.

Pelz(-e) m.   *fur*
Im Winter tragen elegante Damen gerne einen Pelz.
Elegant ladies like to wear fur coats in winter.

Pension(-en) f.   *bed and breakfast*
Pensionen sind oft gemütlicher als Hotels.
Bed and breakfasts are often more cozy than hotels.

Pensionist(-en) m. **Pensionistin(-nen)** f.   *retiree*
Herr Bonesch ist Pensionist und sitzt den ganzen Tag im Park.
Mr. Bonesch is a retiree and spends the whole day sitting in the park.

Perle(-n) f.   *pearl*
Nicole trägt eine schöne Kette aus Perlen.
Nicole is wearing a beautiful pearl necklace.

Perücke(-n) f.   *wig*
Frau Stiegler trägt eine rote Perücke.
Ms. Stiegler is wearing a red wig.

Pessach n.   *Passover*
Pessach ist ein wichtiger Feiertag im Judentum.
Passover is an important holiday in Judaism.

Pfanne(-en) f.   *pan*
Er macht sich ein Spiegelei in der Pfanne.
He is cooking sunny side up eggs in a pan.

Pfeffermühle(-n) f.   *pepper mill*
Die Pfeffermühle steht auf dem Tisch.
The pepper mill is on the table.

Pfeife(-n) f.   *pipe*
Herr Schüssel raucht am Nachmittag gern seine Pfeife im Garten.
Mr. Schüssel likes to smoke his pipe in his garden in the afternoon.

pfeifen   *whistle*
Der Schäfer pfeift seine Hunde herbei.
The shepherd whistles for his dogs to come to him.

Pfingsten n.   *Pentecost*
Pfingsten ist ein wichtiger christlicher Feiertag im Frühling.
Pentecost is an important Christian holiday in spring.

Pflanze(-n) f.   *plant*
Im Garten haben wir sehr schöne exotische Pflanzen.
We have very beautiful exotic plants in the garden.

pflanzen   *to plant*
Im Frühling pflanzen wir Tomaten.
We plant tomatoes in spring.

Pflaster m.   *bandage*
Sie hat sich versehentlich geschnitten und gibt jetzt ein Pflaster
auf die Wunde.
She accidentally cut herself and is putting a bandage on her wound.

Pflicht(-en) f.   *duty*
Jeder Bürger hat die Pflicht, die Steuer zu bezahlen.
It is every citizen's duty to pay taxes.

pflücken   *to pluck*
Die Kinder pflücken Blumen auf der Wiese.
The children pluck flowers in the meadow.

pflügen   *to plow*
Der Bauer pflügt sein Feld.
The farmer plows his field.

pfui   *yuck*
Pfui! Du hast schon wieder nicht dein Zimmer aufgeräumt.
Yuck! You didn't clean up your room once again.

Pfütze(-n) f.   *puddle*
Achtung, nicht in in die Pfütze treten!
Watch out, don't step in the puddle!

Philosophie(-n) f.   *philosophy*
Er hat an der Universität Philosophie studiert.
He studied philosophy at the university.

Physik f.   *physics*
Die Physik ist eine Naturwissenschaft.
Physics is a natural science.

pilgern   *to make a pilgrimage*
Die Gruppe pilgert einmal im Jahr nach Mariazell.
The group makes a pilgrimage to Mariazell once a year.

Pinnwand(-wände) f.   *bulletin board*
Er steckt einen Zettel an die Pinnwand.
He sticks a note on the bulletin board.

Pinsel m. *paintbrush*
Er malt ein Bild mit einem Pinsel.
He paints a picture with a paintbrush.

PKW(-s) m. *car*
Auf dieser Straße dürfen keine PKWs geparkt werden.
No cars can be parked on this street.

Plakat(-e) n. *poster*
Auf dem Plakat wird für ein neues Produkt geworben.
A new product is being advertised on the poster.

Platte(-n) f. *platter*
Jutta serviert verschiedene Würste auf einer Platte.
Jutta is serving assorted sausages on a platter.

Platz(Plätze) m. *place*
Der Tierpark Schönbrunn ist einer der schönsten Plätze in Wien.
The Schönbrunn Zoo is one of the nicest places in Vienna.

plötzlich *suddenly*
Plötzlich hat es angefangen zu schneien, und das mussten wir
vorsichtig weiterfahren.
Suddenly it started to snow and we had to continue driving carefully.

Polen n. *Poland*
Polen liegt östlich von Deutschland.
Poland is located east of Germany.

Politik f. *politics*
Viele Bürger sind mit der Politik unzufrieden.
Many citizens are unhappy with politics.

Politiker m. **Politikerin(-nen)** f. *politician*
Die Politiker halten nicht immer ihre Versprechen.
Politicians don't always keep their promises.

Polizei f. *police*
Die Polizei verfolgt den Verbrecher.
The police are pursuing the criminal.

Polizze(-n) f. *policy*
Die Polizze dieser Versicherung gefällt mir sehr.
I really like this insurance policy.

polnisch *Polish*
Er interessiert sich für die polnische Literatur.
He is interested in Polish literature.

Polster(Pölster) m. *pillow*
Auf dem Sofa gibt es drei große Pölster.
There are three big pillows on the couch.

Porträt(-s) n. *portrait*
Der Maler hat ein Porträt des Präsidenten angefertigt.
The painter painted a portrait of the president.

Porzellan n. *porcelain*
Die große Schüssel ist aus Porzellan.
The big bowl is made of porcelain.

postalisch *by mail*
Den Brief sende ich Ihnen postalisch zu.
I will mail you the letter by mail.

Postamt(-ämter) n. *post office*
Auf dem Postamt kann man Briefe und Pakete aufgeben.
You can mail letters and packages at the post office.

Posten m. *position*
Er hat einen guten Posten bei einer großen Firma bekommen.
He got a good position at a large company.

Postfach(-fächer) n. *post office box*
Viele Firmen haben Postfächer in Liechtenstein.
Many companies have post office boxes in Liechtenstein.

Postkarte(-n) f. *postcard*
Es ist höflich, den Freunden aus dem Urlaub Postkarten zu
senden.
It is polite to mail postcards to your friends while you are on vacation.

Pracht f. *splendor*
Wir sind von der Pracht des Schloss Schönbrunn begeistert.
We are fascinated by the splendor of Schönbrunn Palace.

prachtvoll *magnificent*
Wir haben eine prachtvolle Wohnung in der Wiener Innenstadt
gekauft.
We bought a magnificent apartment in downtown Vienna.

Präsident(-en) m. **Präsidentin(-nen)** f. *president*
Der Präsident ist das Staatsoberhaupt der Vereinigten Staaten
von Amerika.
The president is the head of state of the United States of America.

Preis(-e) m.   *price*
Die Preise sind letztes Jahr wieder stark gestiegen.
The prices greatly increased this past year.

Presse f.   *press*
Die Presse hat ausführlich über den Skandal berichtet.
The press reported extensively on the scandal.

prima   *great*
In diesem Gasthaus habe ich eine prima Pizza gegessen.
I ate a fantastic pizza at this inn.

Prinz(-en) m.   *prince*
Der Prinz führt das schöne Mädchen auf den Ball.
The prince leads the pretty girl to the ball.

Prinzessin(-nen) f.   *princess*
Die Prinzessin wohnt in einem schönen Schloss.
The princess lives in a pretty palace.

privat   *personal*
Ich habe ein privates und ein Geschäftskonto.
I have a personal and a business account.

Produkt(-e) n.   *product*
Unsere Firma produziert verschiedene Produkte aus der
    Stahlindustrie.
Our company produces various products in the steel industry.

Profi(-s) m.   *expert*
Herr Pröll ist ein Profi auf seinem Gebiet der Forschung.
Mr. Pröll is an expert in his area of research.

Programm(-e) n.   *program*
Diesen Herbst bietet das Stadttheater wieder ein interessantes
    Programm an.
*The city theater is offering an interesting program once again
    this fall.*

Prüfung(-en) f.   *exam*
Die Studenten haben große Angst vor der kommenden Prüfung.
The students are very afraid of the coming exam.

Pulver n.   *powder*
Mit diesem Pulver kann man Limonade machen.
You can make lemonade with this powder.

pünktlich   *punctual*
Die Eisenbahn in Deutschland ist nicht immer pünktlich.
The railroad in Germany is not always punctual.

Pünktlichkeit(-en) f.   *punctuality*
Auf Pünktlichkeit wird in Österreich, Deutschland und der
    Schweiz großen Wert gelegt.
Punctuality is very important in Austria, Germany, and Switzerland.

Puppe(-n) f.   *doll*
Das Mädchen spielt mit ihrer Puppe.
The girl plays with her doll.

putzen   *to clean*
Am Sonntag putzt die ganze Familie die Wohnung.
The whole family cleans the apartment on Sunday.

Pyramide(-n) f.   *pyramid*
Viele Touristen fliegen nach Ägypten, um die Pyramiden zu
    sehen.
Many tourists fly to Egypt to see the pyramids.

Q

Qual(-en) f.   *pain*
Die Reise war eine Qual wegen der vielen Verspätungen im
    Flugverkehr.
The trip was a pain because of the many air traffic delays.

Qualität(-en) f.   *quality*
Diese Firma liefert immer die beste Qualität in ihrer Arbeit.
This company always provides the best quality in their work.

Quantität(-en) f.   *quantity*
Qualität geht bei uns in der Production vor Quantität vor.
We value quality over quantity in our production.

quatschen   *to chat*
Die Schüler quatschen während des Unterrichts.
The students are chatting during the lesson.

Quelle(-n) f.   *source, spring*
Die Quelles für dieses Mineralwasser befindet sich in
    Niederösterreich.
The spring for this mineral water is located in Lower Austria.

quer *diagonal*
Hans fährt quer durch die Stadt.
Hans drives diagonally through the town.

Quittung(-en) f. *receipt*
Der Kunde bekommt eine Quittung vom Kellner.
The customer receives a receipt from the waiter.

R

Rabatt(-e) m. *discount*
Wir haben bei unserem Einkauf einen guten Rabatt bekommen.
We got a nice discount on our purchase.

Rache f. *revenge*
Er hat Rache auf den Mörder seiner Schwester verübt.
He took revenge on his sister's murderer.

Rad(Räder) n. *wheel*
Der Wagen hat vier Räder.
The car has four wheels.

radfahren *to bike*
Am Wochenende fahren wir gern rad.
We like to bike on the weekend.

Radfahrer m. **Radfahrerin(-nen)** f. *bicyclist*
Radfahrer dürfen nicht auf der Autobahn fahren.
Bicyclists are not allowed to drive on the highway.

Radio(-s) n. *radio*
Margarethe hört morgens gern Radio.
Margarethe likes to listen to the radio in the morning.

Rakete(-n) f. *rocket*
Das Militär feuert eine Rakete während eines Manövers.
The military fires a rocket during a maneuver.

Ramadan m. *Ramadan*
Der Ramadan ist ein wichtiger Feiertag im Islam.
Ramadan is an important holiday in Islam.

Rappen m. *centime (Switzerland)*
Jeder Schweizer Franken hat 100 Rappen.
Every Swiss franc has 100 centimes.

Rasen m.   *lawn*
Günther mäht jeden Freitag den Rasen.
Günther mows the lawn every Friday.

Rat m.   *advice*
Der Patient bittet den Arzt um Rat.
The patient asks the physician for advice.

Rathaus(-häuser) n.   *city hall*
Der Bürgermeister arbeitet im Rathaus.
The mayor works in city hall.

ratsam   *advisable*
Bei Auslandsreisen ist es ratsam, sich über die
    Einreisebestimmungen des Ziellandes zu informieren.
*When traveling abroad, it is advisable to know the destination country's
    entry requirements.*

Rauch m.   *smoke*
Das Lagerfeuer hat viel Rauch verursacht.
The campfire caused a lot of smoke.

rauchen   *to smoke*
Weil es nicht gesund ist, rauchen heute weniger Leute als
    früher.
Because it is not healthy, fewer people smoke today than in the past.

Raucher m. **Raucherin(-nen)** f.   *smoker*
Raucher dürfen hier nicht sitzen.
Smokers may not sit here.

raufen   *to fight*
Die zwei Jungen haben in der Pause gerauft und mussten
    deswegen nach Hause.
*The two boys fought during the break and that is why they had to
    go home.*

Raum(Räume) m.   *space*
Wir sind in ein neues Haus gezogen, weil wir mehr Raum
    brauchten.
We moved to a new house because we needed more room.

rauschen   *to rustle*
Die Blätter rauschen im Wind.
The leaves rustle in the wind.

rechnen   *to calculate, to do math*
In der Volksschule lernen die Kinder rechnen.
Children learn math in elementary school.

Rechnung(-en) f.   *bill*
Wenn man im Restaurant mit dem Essen fertig ist, bekommt
   man die Rechnung.
When you are done eating at a restaurant, you get the bill.

Recht(-e) n.   *right*
Das Recht auf freie Meinungsäußerung ist stärker in den USA als
   in Deutschland.
*The right of freedom of speech is more strongly enforced in the U.S.A.
   than in Germany.*

reden   *to talk*
Herr Kirchschläger redet gern mit seinen Nachbarn.
Mr. Kirchschläger likes to talk with his neighbors.

Regel(-n) f.   *rule*
Er hält sich beim Schachspielen nicht immer an die Regeln.
He does not always follow the rules when playing chess.

regeln   *to settle, to resolve*
Wie regeln wir den Konflikt?
How do we resolve the conflict?

Regen m.   *rain*
Der Regen war gestern ganz besonders stark.
The rain was especially strong yesterday.

Regenbogen m.   *rainbow*
Nach dem Gewitter haben wir einen schönen Regenbogen gesehen.
After the thunderstorm, we saw a beautiful rainbow.

Regenschirm(-e) m.   *umbrella*
Da sie ihren Regenschirm vergessen hat, ist sie nass geworden.
Because she forgot her umbrella, she got wet.

regieren   *to rule*
Liechtenstein wird von einem Fürsten regiert.
Liechtenstein is ruled by a prince.

Regierung(-en) f.   *government*
Die Regierung hat beschlossen, die Steuern zu erhöhen.
The government has decided to raise taxes.

regnen   *to rain*
> Morgen können wir nicht im Wald wandern, denn es soll regnen.
> *We can't go hiking in the forest tomorrow because it is supposed to rain.*

Reformationstag m.   *Reformation Day*
> Der Reformationstag ist ein wichtiger Feiertag für die Evangelen in Deutschland.
> *Reformation Day is an important holiday for Protestants in Germany.*

reich   *rich*
> Die Schweiz ist ein reiches Land.
> *Switzerland is a rich country.*

Reich(-e) n.   *empire*
> Das Osmanische Reich war ein Land im Südosten Europas.
> *The Ottoman Empire was a country in Southeastern Europe.*

Reichtum(-tümer) m.   *richness*
> Ich kenne den Reichtum der deutschsprachigen Kultur.
> *I know the richness of German-speaking culture.*

reif   *mature*
> Dieser Schüler ist reifer als die anderen.
> *This student is more mature than the others.*

Reifen m.   *tire*
> Die Reifen müssen bei diesem Wagen gewechselt werden.
> *The tires on this car need to be changed.*

rein   *clean*
> Das Messer ist rein.
> *The knife is clean.*

reinigen   *to clean*
> Frau Vukovic reinigt das Badezimmer.
> *Ms. Vukovic is cleaning the bathroom.*

Reiniger m.   *cleaner*
> Er kauft im Geschäft einen Reiniger fürs Badezimmer.
> *He buys a bathroom cleaner at the store.*

Reise(-n) f.   *trip*
> Nächstes Jahr machen die Klestils eine Reise nach Kanada.
> *Next year the Klestils will take a trip to Canada.*

Reisebüro(-s) n.   *travel agency*
> Im Reisebüro kann man Reisen buchen.
> *You can book trips at a travel agency.*

reisen *to travel*
Die Familie Schmidt reist in den Ferien nach Spanien.
The Schmidt family is traveling to Spain during their vacation.

Reisepass(-pässe) m. *passport*
Einen Reisepass braucht man, um eine internationale Grenze zu
überschreiten.
You need a passport to cross an international border.

Reparatur(-en) f. *repair*
Die Reparatur des Kühlschranks hat viel gekostet.
The refrigerator repair was expensive.

reparieren *to repair*
Das Auto wird in der Werkstatt repariert.
The car is being repaired in the workshop.

Republik(-en) f. *republic*
Österreich ist eine Republik.
Austria is a republic.

retten *to rescue*
Die Feuerwehrleute retteten die Katze aus dem brennenden
Haus.
The firemen rescued the cat from the burning house.

Retter m. *rescuer*
Die Retter wurden vom Bürgermeister in einer Zeremonie
geehrt.
The rescuers were honored by the mayor at a ceremony.

Rezept(-e) n. *recipe*
Das Rezept für die Speckknödel muss ich unbedingt haben.
I absolutely must have the recipe for the bacon dumplings.

richten *to fix*
Er hat mir den Kühlschrank gerichtet.
He fixed the fridge.

richtig *correct*
Der Kandidat hat im Quiz alle Fragen richtig beantwortet.
The quiz show candidate answered all the questions correctly.

Richtung(-en) f. *direction*
Fahren Sie etwa 200 km in Richtung Rostock.
Drive about 200 kilometers in the direction of Rostock.

riechen   *to smell*
Hier riecht es aber nicht gut!
It does not smell good here!

Ring(-e) m.   *ring*
Bei der Hochzeit tauschten die Eheleute Ringe aus.
The bride and groom exchanged rings at their wedding.

ringen   *to wrestle*
Das ist ein Problem, mit dem wir noch eine Weile ringen werden.
This is a problem we will have to wrestle with for a little while longer.

Ritter m.   *knight*
Im Mittelalter lebten Ritter auf Burgen.
In the Middle Ages, knights lived in castles.

Rolltreppe(-n) f.   *escalator*
Mit der Rolltreppe kann man von einem Stock in den anderen fahren.
You can travel from one floor to another on the escalator.

Roman(-e) m.   *novel*
Er liest einen interessanten Roman von Christa Wolf.
He is reading an interesting novel by Christa Wolf.

röntgen   *to x-ray*
Nach dem Unfall hat er Schmerzen im Arm und der Arzt lässt den Arm deswegen röntgen.
He had pain in his arm after the accident; therefore, the doctor is having his arm x-rayed.

Rückgeld(-er) n.   *change*
Die Verkäuferin gibt ihm 75 Cent Rückgeld.
The sales person gives him 75 cents back as change.

Rucksack(-säcke) m.   *backpack*
Er trägt die Bücher in einem Rucksack.
He carries the books in a backpack.

rückwärts   *backwards*
Der Wagen rollt rückwärts die Straße hinunter.
The car is rolling backwards down the street.

rufen   *to call*
Der Vater ruft seine Kinder herbei.
The father calls for his children to come to him.

rügen   *to reprimand*
Der Lehrer rügt den Schüler für dessen schlechtes Benehmen.
The teacher reprimands the student for his bad behavior.

Ruhe f.   *quiet*
Um ihre Arbeit zu schreiben, brauchen die Studenten viel Ruhe.
The students needs lots of peace and quiet to complete their exams.

ruhig   *quiet*
Eva ist ein ruhiges Kind und macht nur selten Lärm.
Eva is a quiet child and seldom makes noise.

Rutsche(-n) f.   *slide*
Die Kinder spielen vergnügt auf der Rutsche.
The children are playing joyfully on the slide.

rutschen   *to slide, slip*
Wenn man im Winter keine guten Schuhe trägt, kann man auf
dem Glatteis rutschen.
If you don't wear good shoes in winter, you can slip on the ice.

S

Saal(Säle) m.   *hall*
Das Fest hat im großen Saal stattgefunden.
The party took place in the large hall.

Sache(-n) f.   *thing*
Schifahren ist eine prima Sache.
Skiing is a awesome thing.

Sackerl(-n) n.   *shopping bag (in Austria)*
Sabine bringt ihre Einkäufe in einem Sackerl nach Hause.
Sabine is bringing her purchases home in a shopping bag.

säen   *to sow*
Der Bauer sät sein Feld.
The farmer sows his field.

sägen   *to saw*
Die Arbeiter sägen am Baum.
The workers are sawing the tree.

Salbe(-n) f.   *ointment*
Der Arzt verschreibt eine Salbe für die Wunde.
The doctor prescribes an ointment for the wound.

sammeln   *to collect*
Sie sammelt Postkarten aus dem Urlaub.
She collects postcards while on vacation.

Sammlung(-en) f.   *collection*
In der Sammlung des Museums befinden sich viele kostbare
   Gemälde.
There are many precious paintings in the museum's collection.

Sand m.   *sand*
Die Kinder bauen eine Burg aus dem Sand am Strand.
The children are building a sand castle on the beach.

Sandale(-n) f.   *sandals*
Im Sommer trägt er immer Sandalen.
He always wears sandals in summer.

sauer   *sour*
Die Milch war nicht im Kühlschrank und jetzt ist sie sauer.
The milk was not in the fridge and now it is sour.

Sauerstoff(-e) m.   *oxygen*
Der Patient bekommt Sauerstoff zum Atmen.
The patient receives oxygen in order to breathe.

S-Bahn(-en) f.   *commuter train*
Mit der S-Bahn kann man von Berlin nach Potsdam fahren.
You can take the commuter train from Berlin to Potsdam.

Schach n.   *chess*
Wir spielen gern Schach mit unseren Freunden.
We like to play chess with our friends.

Schachtel(-n) f.   *box*
Am Valentinstag habe ich eine Schachtel Pralinen bekommen.
I got a box of chocolates on Valentine's Day.

Schaden(Schäden) m.   *damage*
Der Regen hat viel Schaden in der Landwirtschaft verursacht.
The rain caused a lot of damage to agriculture.

schädlich   *harmful*
Rauchen ist sehr schädlich für die Gesundheit.
Smoking is very harmful to your health.

Schalter m.   *switch*
Am Schalter kannst du das Licht andrehen.
You can turn on the light with the switch.

scharf *sharp*
Wir haben ein scharfes Messer in der Küche.
We have a sharp knife in the kitchen.

Schatten m. *shadow, shade*
Wenn es heiß ist, sitzen wir gern im Schatten.
When it is hot outside, we like to sit in the shade.

schattig *shady*
Im Garten haben wir einen schönen schattigen Platz.
In the yard we have a nice shady area.

Schaukel(-n) f. *swing*
Die Kinder spielen auf der Schaukel.
The children play on the swing.

schauen *to look*
Sie schaut sich die Flugzeuge am Flughafen an.
She looks at the airplanes at the airport.

Schaufel(-n) f. *shovel*
Er grabt mit der Schaufel ein Loch in der Erde.
He digs a hole in the soil with a shovel.

Schaum(Schäume) m. *foam*
Auf jedem Glas Bier gibt es immer eine Schicht Schaum.
In every glass of beer there is always a layer of foam.

Schaumbad(-bäder) n. *bubble bath*
Marianne entspannt sich in einem warmen Schaumbad.
Marianne relaxes in a warm bubble bath.

Scheck(-s) m. *check*
Frau Pamuk stellt ihrem Sohn einen Scheck für 200 Euro aus.
Ms. Pamuk writes her son a check for 200 euros.

Scheibe(-n) f. *slice*
Atahan schmiert Leberwurst auf eine Scheibe Brot.
Atahan spreads liverwurst on a slice of bread.

scheiden *to divorce*
Das Paar hat sich schon vor Jahren geschieden.
The couple divorced years ago.

Schein m. *shine*
Sie kann sich im Schein des Wagens spiegeln.
She can see herself reflected in the shine of the car.

Scheinwerfer m.   *headlight*
   Die Scheinwerfer bei diesem Wagen sind einfach zu hell.
   The headlights on this car are simply too bright.

schenken   *to give a gift*
   Zum Geburtstag schenke ich meiner Frau Blumen.
   I give my wife flowers for her birthday.

Schere(-n) f.   *scissors*
   Die Friseurin schneidet Haare mit einer Schere.
   The hairdresser cuts hair with a pair of scissors.

Scherz(-e) m.   *joke*
   Das kann doch nicht wahr sein. Das ist ein Scherz.
   That can't be true. It's a joke.

Schicht(-en) f.   *layer*
   Die oberste Schicht der Torte besteht aus Schlagobers und
      Erdbeeren.
   The top layer of the torte consists of whipped cream and strawberries.

schicken   *to send*
   Der Junge schickt einen Brief an seine Großmutter.
   The boy sends a letter to his grandmother.

Schicksal(-e) n.   *fate*
   Das Schicksal hat es nicht gut mit Mozart gemeint, denn er ist
      jung gestorben.
   Fate was not kind to Mozart, as he died young.

schieben   *to push*
   Er schiebt seinen Wagen, weil er nicht starten wollte.
   He is pushing his car because it did not want to start.

schifahren   *to ski*
   Das ganze Jahr über kann man in Tirol schifahren.
   You can ski in Tyrol all year round.

Schiff(-e) n.   *ship*
   Auf diesem schönen großen Schiff gibt es über 300 Kabinen.
   There are over 300 cabins on this large ship.

Schiffsreise(-n) f.   *voyage, cruise*
   Sie macht eine Schiffsreise nach Norwegen.
   She is taking a cruise to Norway.

Schild(-er) n.   *sign, placard*
Auf dem Schild steht, dass das Betreten des Rasens verboten ist.
It says on the sign that stepping on the lawn is prohibited.

schimpfen   *to rant*
Er schimpft auf die Politiker, weil er mit der Regierung nicht
   zufrieden ist.
*He rants about the politicians because he is not happy with the
   government.*

Schirm(-e) m.   *umbrella*
Bitte bring einen Schirm mit, denn es könnte regnen.
Please bring an umbrella because it could rain.

Schlacht(-en) f.   *battle*
Auf diesem Feld hat es vor 200 Jahren eine große Schlacht
   gegeben.
There was a big battle on this field 200 years ago.

schlachten   *to slaughter*
Der Fleischhauer schlachtet die Schweine.
The butcher slaughters the pigs.

schlafen   *to sleep*
Wir schlafen am besten, wenn es draußen ruhig ist.
We sleep best when it is quiet outside.

Schlafwagen m.   *sleeping car*
In Europa kann man noch auf einigen Strecken mit dem
   Schlafwagen fahren.
In Europe you can still travel on a sleeping car on some routes.

Schlag(Schläge) m.   *hit*
Der arme Hund hat von seinem Besitzer einen Schlag
   bekommen.
The poor dog was hit by his owner.

Schlager m.   *hit song*
Edeltraud hört gern österreichische und deutsche Schlager
   im Radio.
Edeltraud likes to hear Austrian and German hit songs on the radio.

Schlamassel m.   *mess*
Jetzt haben wir den Schlamassel, weil du nicht vorsichtig warst.
Now we have a mess because you were not careful.

schlecht   *bad*
Mit dieser Fluglinie haben wir schlechte Erfahrungen gemacht.
We have had bad experiences with this airline.

schleichen   *to sneak*
Der Sohn schleicht nach Mitternacht durch die Wohnung, um die
Eltern nicht zu wecken.
*In order not to wake his parents, the son sneaks through the apartment
after midnight.*

schleppen   *to haul*
Sie schleppt ihre Koffer zum Flughafen.
She is hauling her suitcases to the airport.

schließen   *to close*
Am Sonntag sind alle Geschäfte in Deutschland, Österreich und
der Schweiz geschlossen.
All stores in Germany, Austria, and Switzerland are closed on Sunday.

Schlitten m.   *sled*
In den Alpen kann man auch mit dem Schlitten fahren.
You can ride on a sled in the Alps.

Schloss(Schlösser) n.   *palace*
In Frankreich kann man viele berühmte Schlösser besuchen.
You can visit many famous palaces in France

schlucken   *to swallow*
Er schluckt eine Tablette.
He swallows a pill.

schlürfen   *to slurp*
Er schlürft langsam die Suppe.
He slowly slurps the soup.

Schlüssel m.   *key*
Er hat die Schlüssel für das Büro zu Hause vergessen.
He forgot his office keys at home.

Schlüsselbund(-bunde) m.   *key chain*
Er hat alle seine Schlüssel auf dem gleichen Schlüsselbund.
He has all his keys on the same key chain.

Schmankerl(-n) n.   *delicacy*
Eine frische Leberkäsesemmel gehört zu den Schmankerln der
bayrischen Küche.
A fresh liver-cheese roll is one of the delicacies of Bavarian cuisine.

schmecken *to taste, to enjoy eating*
Den Kindern in Wien schmecken Topfengolatschen
besonders gut.
Children in Vienna especially enjoy eating cheese pastries.

schmelzen *to melt*
Für ein Käsefondue in der Schweiz muss man Käse in einem
Topf schmelzen.
In Switzerland, you need to melt cheese in a pot for cheese fondue.

Schmerz(-en) m. *pain*
Seit dem Unfall hat er Schmerzen in seinem Bein.
He has had pain in his leg since the accident.

schmieren *to spread*
Er schmiert sich Butter auf das Brot.
He is spreading butter on the bread.

Schminke f. *makeup*
Ohne Schminke geht Frau Meyer nicht gern aus dem Haus.
Ms. Meyer does not like to leave the house without makeup.

schminken *to put on makeup*
In der Früh schminkt sie sich vor dem Spiegel.
She puts on her makeup in front of the mirror in the morning.

schmollen *to pout*
Das Kind schmollt mit den Eltern, weil es kein Geschenk
bekommen hat.
The child pouts at his parents because he did not get a gift.

Schmuck m. *jewelry*
Er hat seiner Frau Schmuck zum Geburtstag geschenkt.
He gave his wife jewelry for her birthday.

schmusen *to cuddle*
Die zwei schmusen in der Ecke.
The two are cuddling in the corner of the room.

Schmutz m. *dirt*
Das Zimmer ist voller Schmutz.
The room is full of dirt.

schmutzig *dirty*
Er wäscht die schmutzigen Socken.
He washes his dirty socks.

schnarchen   *snore*
Er schnarchte die ganze Nacht, sodass seine Frau nicht schlafen konnte.
He snored all night and his wife could not sleep.

schnäuzen   *to blow one's nose*
Er hat einen Schnupfen und muss sich oft schäuzen.
He has a cold and has to blow his nose often.

schneiden   *to cut*
Hugo schneidet sich eine Scheibe Brot.
Hugo cuts a slice of bread.

schneien   *to snow*
In den Alpen kann es auf Berggipfeln auch im Sommer schneien.
It can even snow in summer on the mountain tops in the Alps.

schnell   *quickly*
Er ist zu schnell auf der Autobahn gefahren und hat einen Strafzettel bekommen.
He drove too quickly on the highway and got a speeding ticket.

Schnitt(-e) m.   *cut*
Der Schnitt der Hose ist zu eng.
The cut of the pants is too narrow.

Schnuller m.   *pacifier*
Das Baby schreit nicht, weil es einen Schnuller im Mund hat.
The baby doesn't scream because there is a pacifier in its mouth.

Schnupfen m.   *cold*
Der Lehrer hat einen Schnupfen und bringt Taschentücher in die Klasse.
The teacher has a cold and brings tissues to class.

schon   *already*
Ich bin schon in Bern angekommen.
I have already arrived in Bern.

schön   *beautiful*
Bern ist eine schöne Stadt in der Schweiz.
Bern is a beautiful city in Switzerland.

Schönheit(-en) f.   *beauty*
Schönheit vergeht mit der Jugend.
Beauty passes with youth.

Schrank(Schränke) m.   *cabinet*
Er stellt die Gläser in den Schrank.
He puts the glasses in the cabinet.

Schranke(-n) f.   *gate*
Der Schranken ist geschlossen und die Autofahrer müssen
warten, bis der Zug vorbeifährt.
The gate is closed and the drivers have to wait until the train passes.

Schraube(-n) f.   *screw*
Es fehlt eine Schraube in diesem Tisch.
There is a screw missing in this table.

Schraubenzieher m.   *screwdriver*
Mit dem Schraubenzieher kann man Schrauben festziehen.
You can screw in screws with a screwdriver.

Schrecken m.   *scare*
Die Überlebenden sind mit dem Schrecken davon gekommen.
The survivors got away with a scare.

schrecklich   *terrible*
Sie hat gerade die schrecklichen Nachrichten im Radio gehört.
She just heard the terrible news on the radio.

schreiben   *to write*
Der Reporter schreibt einen interessanten Bericht für die Zeitung.
The reporter is writing an interesting article for the newspaper.

Schreibtisch(-e) m.   *desk*
Sie schreibt auf ihrem Laptop auf dem Schreibtisch.
She writes on her laptop on the desk.

schreien   *to scream*
Die Jugendlichen schreien, wenn sie mit der Achterbahn fahren.
The teenagers scream when they ride the rollercoaster.

Schrift(-en) f.   *writing*
Diese Schrift ist nicht leicht zu entziffern.
It isn't easy to decipher this writing.

Schriftsteller m. **Schriftstellerin(-nen)** f.   *writer*
Thomas Mann war einer der größten deutschen Schriftsteller
des 20. Jahrhunderts.
*Thomas Mann was one of the greatest German writers of the 20th
century.*

Schritt(-e) m.   *step*
Er nimmt einen Schritt nach dem anderen, um nicht zu fallen.
He takes one step at a time so he won't fall.

schrumpfen   *to shrink*
Der Pullover ist in der Waschmaschine geschrumpft.
The sweatshirt shrunk in the washing machine.

Schuld(-en) f.   *guilt, debt*
Er trägt die Schuld für den Unfall.
He bears the guilt for the accident.

Schule(-n) f.   *school*
Veronika geht gern in die Schule.
Veronika likes to go to school.

Schüler m. **Schülerin(-nen)** f.   *students (K-12), pupils*
Die Schüler hören der Lehrerin aufmerksam zu.
The students listen attentively to their teacher.

schummeln   *to cheat*
Er schummelt leider beim Karten spielen.
Unfortunately, he cheats when he plays cards.

Schürze(-n) f.   *apron*
Beim Kochen trägt er immer eine Schürze.
He always wears an apron while cooking.

Schüssel(-n) f.   *bowl*
Er trinkt die Suppe aus der Schüssel.
He drinks the soup from the bowl.

Schutz m.   *protection*
Der Zeuge steht unter Schutz der Polizei.
The witness is under police protection.

schwach   *weak*
Das ist ein schwacher Film, der mich nicht unterhalten hat.
This is a weak film that did not entertain me.

schwanger   *pregnant*
Sie ist im dritten Monat schwanger.
She is three months pregnant.

Schwangerschaft(-en) f.   *pregnancy*
Sie freut sich über ihre Schwangerschaft.
She is excited about her pregnancy.

schwärmen   *to rave*
Wir schwärmen von unserem Urlaub in Israel.
We are raving about our vacation in Israel.

Schweden n.   *Sweden*
Herr Anderson kommt aus Stockholm und wohnt in Schweden.
Mr. Anderson comes from Sweden and lives in Sweden

schwedisch   *Swedish*
Er schwärmt von der schwedischen Küche.
He raves about Swedish cuisine.

Schweiß m.   *sweat*
Da es so heiß ist, steht ihm der Scheiß auf der Stirn.
Because it is so hot, he has sweat on his forehead.

Schweiz f.   *Switzerland*
Die Schweiz ist ein neutrales Land mitten in der Europäischen Union.
Switzerland is a neutral country in the middle of the European Union.

Schweizer m. **Schweizerin(-nen)** f.   *Swiss person*
Herr Neiger ist Schweizer und kommt aus Interlaken.
Mr. Neiger is Swiss and comes from Interlaken.

schweizerisch   *Swiss*
Wo finde ich das schweizerische Konsulat?
Where do I find the Swiss Consulate?

schwierig   *difficult*
Das ist ein schwieriges Problem, auf das ich keine Lösung kenne.
This is a difficult problem that I don't know the solution to.

Schwimmbad(-bäder) n.   *swimming pool*
Im Sommer gehen die Kinder gern ins Schwimmbad.
Children like to go to the swimming pool during the summer.

schwimmen   *to swim*
Die Berliner schwimmen gern im Wannsee.
Berliners like to swim in Lake Wannsee.

schwitzen   *to sweat*
Diese Hitze ist sehr unangenehm, weil man so viel schmitzen muss.
This heat is very unpleasant because you sweat so much.

schwören   *swear*
Die Soldaten schwören einen Eid auf die Verfassung.
The soldiers swear an oath on the constitution.

schwul   *gay*
Peter und Jochen sind ein schwules Paar.
Peter and Jochen are a gay couple.

schwül   *humid*
Die Luft ist heute ganz besonders schwül.
The air is exceptionally humid today.

Schwule(-en) m.   *gay person*
Diese Organisation unterstützt gleiche Rechte für Schwule.
This organization supports equal rights for gay people.

See(-n) m.   *lake*
In Österreich gibt es in den Bergen viele schöne Seen.
There are many beautiful lakes in the Austrian mountains.

sehen   *to see*
Er hat gestern den Sonnenaufgang gesehen.
He saw the sunrise yesterday.

sehenswürdig   *worth seeing*
In Wien gibt es viele sehenswürdige Gebäude.
There are many buildings worth seeing in Vienna.

Sehenswürdigkeit(-en) f.   *sight*
Das Brandenburger Tor in Berlin ist wohl eine der bedeutendsten Sehenwürdigkeiten Deutschlands.
The Brandenburg Gate in Berlin is one of the most significant sights in Germany.

Sehnsucht(-süchte) f.   *longing*
Paul hat große Sehnsucht nach den sonnigen Stränden Spaniens.
Paul has great longing for the sunny beaches of Spain.

sehr   *very*
Nach einem langen Tag ist er jetzt sehr müde.
After a long day, he is very tired.

Seide f.   *silk*
Der gelbe Schal ist aus reiner Seide.
The yellow scarf is made of pure silk.

Seife(-n) f.   *soap*
Er kauft Seife in der Drogerie.
He buys soap at the drugstore.

Seifenblase(-n) f.   *soap bubble*
Die Kinder spielen gern mit Seifenblasen im Park.
The children like to play with soap bubbles in the park.

Seil(-e) n.   *rope*
Der Junge klettert auf einem Seil im Turnsaal.
The boy is climbing a rope in the gym.

Seilbahn(-en) f.   *cable car, gondola*
In der Schweiz gibt es viele Seilbahnen, die Wanderer auf die
   Berghöhen befördern.
*In Switzerland, there are many cable cars that take hikers up the
   mountains.*

sein   *to be*
Hans ist Schauspieler am Theater.
Hans is an actor at the theater.

Seite(-n) f.   *page*
Das Buch hat über 200 Seiten.
The book has over 200 pages.

selbst   *himself, herself*
Er hat das Haus selbst gebaut.
He built the house himself.

selbstverständlich   *of course*
Wir fahren selbstverständlich jedes Jahr in Urlaub.
Of course we go on vacation every year.

selten   *seldom*
Wir fahren nur selten nach Bremen.
We seldom go to Bremen.

senden   *to broadcast*
Im Fernsehen haben sie das große Fußballspiel live gesendet.
They broadcasted the big soccer game live on TV.

Sendung(-en) f.   *broadcast program*
Sie sieht gern viele verschiedene Sendungen im Fernsehen.
She likes to watch many different TV programs.

senken   *to lower*
Die Steuern werden nächstes Jahr gesenkt.
Taxes will be lowered next year.

servieren   *to serve*
Der Kellner serviert das Abendessen.
The waiter is serving dinner.

Sessel m.   *chair*
Er sitzt auf einem Sessel in der Küche.
He is sitting on a chair in the kitchen.

setzen   *to put, to sit down*
Kommen Sie bitte herein und setzen Sie sich.
Please come in and sit down.

shoppen   *to go shopping*
Die drei Damen gehen gern im Einkaufszentrum shoppen.
The three ladies like to go shopping at the mall.

sicher   *safe*
Sie fühlt sich zu Hause sehr sicher.
She feels very safe at home.

Sicherheit(-en) f.   *safety*
Wir garantieren die Sicherheit unserer Passagiere.
We guarantee the safety of our passangers.

Sicht(-en) f.   *sight, view*
Von diesem Sitz hat man keine gute Sicht auf die Bühne.
You don't have a good view of the stage from this seat.

sichten   *to sight*
Vom Schiff aus haben wir zwei Wale gesichtet.
We sighted two whales from the ship.

Sichtvermerk(-e) m.   *visa*
Ausländer benötigen für die Einreise in dieses Land einen
     Sichtvermerk.
Foreigners need a visa for entry into this country.

Sieb(-e) n.   *sieve, colander*
Er hat ein Sieb in der Küche.
He has a colander in the kitchen.

Sieg(-e) m.   *victory*
Die Mannschaft hat wieder einen Sieg eingespielt.
The team brought home another victory.

Silber n.   *silver*
Dieser alte Topf ist aus Silber und muss poliert werden.
This old pot is made of silver and needs to be polished.

singen   *to sing*
Während der Messe hat der Kirchenchor so schön gesungen.
The church choir sang so nicely during mass.

Sinn(-e) m.   *sense*
Ich verstehe nicht den Sinn dieser Arbeit.
This work doesn't make sense to me.

sitzen   *sit*
Sie sitzt und wartet auf die Ärztin.
She is sitting and waiting for the doctor.

Skandal(-e) m.   *scandal*
Der Skandal hat die Öffentlichkeit erschüttert.
The scandal shook the public.

Sofa(-s) n.   *couch*
Wir haben ein großes Sofa, auf dem man auch schlafen kann.
We have a large couch that you can also sleep on.

sofort   *immediately*
Ich komme sofort zurück.
I will be back immediately.

sollen   *supposed to*
Der Lehrer hat gesagt, dass ich mehr lernen soll.
The teacher said that I am supposed to study more.

Sonne(-n) f.   *sun*
Im Winter geht die Sonne spät auf und früh unter.
In winter, the sun rises late and sets early.

Sonnenbrand(-brände) m.   *sunburn*
Branko hat so lange in der Sonne gelegen, dass er einen
schlimmen Sonnenbrand bekommen hat.
Branko laid in the sun for so long that he got a bad sunburn.

Sonnenbrille(-n) f.   *sunglasses*
Im Sommer trägt er gern Sonnenbrillen.
He likes to wear sunglasses in summer.

sparen   *to save*
Er spart für einen Urlaub in Südafrika.
He is saving money for a vacation to South Africa.

Sparbuch(-bücher) n.   *savings account*
Die Mutter legt Geld für ihre Kinder in einem Sparbuch an.
The mother deposits money for her children in a savings account.

Spaß(Späße) m.   *fun*
Beim Fest haben alle Spaß gehabt.
Everyone had fun at the party.

spät   *late*
Harald ist schon wieder spät zur Arbeit gekommen.
Harald was late for work again.

spazieren   *to go for a walk*
Am Sonntag gehen viele Leute gern spazieren.
Many people like to go for a walk on Sunday.

Spaziergang(-gänge) m.   *stroll*
Nach dem Spaziergang durch die Stadt hat das Paar im
    Kaffeehaus eine Torte gegessen.
After a stroll through the city, the couple ate a torte at the café.

Speise(-n) f.   *dish, meal*
Die Speisen in diesem Restaurant haben mir sehr gut
    geschmeckt.
I really liked the meals at this restaurant.

Speisekarte(-n) f.   *menu*
Auf der Speisekarte sehe ich ein gutes Wiener Schnitzel.
I see a great wiener schnitzel on the menu.

Spiegel m.   *mirror*
Siegfried schaut in den Spiegel während er sich rasiert.
Siegfried looks in the mirror while he shaves.

spiegeln   *to reflect*
Die Sonne spiegelt sich im See.
The sun is reflected on the lake.

Spiel(-e) n.   *game*
Die Kinder haben heute viele Spiele gespielt.
The children played many games today.

spielen   *to play*
Die Kinder spielen Fußball im Hof.
The children are playing soccer in the yard.

Spielzeug(-e) n.   *toy*
Die Eltern kaufen dem Kind ein neues Spielzeug.
The parents buy their child a new toy.

spitz   *pointy*
Achtung! Das Messer ist sehr spitz.
Be careful! The knife is very pointy.

Spitze(-n) f.   *peak*
Der Bergsteiger hat die Spitze des Mount Everest erklommen.
The mountaineer reached Mount Everest's peak.

Sport(Sportarten) m.   *sport*
Josef mag keinen Sport.
Josef does not like sports.

Sportverein(-e) m.   *sports club*
Fast alle Bewohner des Dorfes sind Mitglieder im Sportverein.
Almost all of the village residents are members of the sports club.

Sprache(-n) f.   *language*
Englisch und Deutsch sind germanische Sprachen.
English and German are Germanic languages.

sprechen   *to speak*
Imre spricht drei Sprachen: Ungarisch, Deutsch und
    Rumänisch.
Imre speaks three languages: Hungarian, German, and Romanian.

springen   *to jump*
Es ist keine gute Idee vom Zug zu springen, bevor er
    angehalten hat.
It isn't a good idea to jump from the train before it has stopped.

spritzen   *to squirt*
Die Kinder spritzen mit dem Wasser im Brunnen.
The children squirt each other with water in the fountain.

Sprühdose(-n) f.   *spray can*
Er hat eine alte rostige Sprühdose im Keller gefunden.
He found an old rusty spray can in the basement.

sprühen   *to spray*
Der Bauer sprüht Insektizide auf das Gemüse.
The farmer sprays insecticides on the vegetables.

Sprung(Sprünge) m.   *jump*
Der Sprung von der Stiege war keine gute Idee, denn Rudi hat
sich dabei weh getan.
*A jump from the staircase was not a good idea because Rudi hurt
himself.*

spülen   *to rinse*
Wir spülen nach dem Abendessen gemeinsam das Geschirr.
We will rinse the dishes together after dinner.

Spülmaschine(-n) f.   *dishwasher*
In der Spülmaschine werden die Gläser gewaschen.
The glasses are being washed in the dishwasher.

Spur(-en) f.   *trace, track*
Die Polizei verfolgt die Spur des Verbrechers.
The police pursue the criminal's tracks.

spüren   *to feel*
Er spürt die Kälte des Regens auf der Haut.
He feels the coldness of the rain on his skin.

Staat(-en) m.   *state*
Luxemburg ist ein unabhängiger Staat in Europa.
Luxembourg is an independent state in Europa.

Staatsbürgerschaft(-en) f.   *citizenship*
Herr Gorbach besitzt die österreichische Staatsbürgerschaft.
Mr. Gorbach has Austrian citizenship.

Staatsoberhaupt(-häupter) m.   *head of state*
Der Präsident ist das Staatsoberhaupt Frankreichs.
The president is the head of state in France.

stachelig   *prickly*
Der Kaktus ist stachelig.
The cactus is prickly.

Stadium(Stadien) n.   *stadium*
Im Stadium hat es ein großes Live-Konzert gegeben.
There was a huge live concert in the stadium.

Stadt(Städte) f.   *city*
Innsbruck ist eine schöne Stadt in Österreich.
Innsbruck is a lovely city in Austria.

Stadtbahn(-en) f.   *light rail*
Mit der Stadtbahn kann man von Düsseldorf bis nach Dortmund
    fahren.
You can take the light rail all the way from Düsseldorf to Dortmund.

Stahl m.   *steel*
Die Brücke ist aus Stahl.
The bridge is made of steel.

Stall(Ställe) m.   *barn*
Im Stall schlafen die Kühe.
The cows are sleeping in the barn.

stammen   *to be from*
Herr Pflamitzer stammt aus Wien.
Mr. Pflamitzer is from Vienna.

Standseilbahn(-en) f.   *incline, cable car*
Auf den Salzburger Mönchsberg fährt man mit der
    Standseilbahn.
Thecable car travels up Salzburg's Mönchsberg.

stark   *strong*
Das ist ein starker Junge, der dir helfen kann, die Koffer zu
    tragen.
This is a strong boy who can help you carry the suitcases.

statt   *instead*
Ich hätte gern einen Salat statt der Pommes Frites.
I would like a salad instead of the french fries.

stattfinden   *to take place*
Das Konzert findet morgen im Theater statt.
The concert will take place in the theater tomorrow.

staunen   *to be amazed*
Sie staunt wie schön das Schloss Sanssouci ist.
She is amazed at how beautiful the Sanssouci Palace is.

stechen   *to sting*
Walter ist von einer Biene gestochen worden.
Walter was stung by a bee.

Steckdose(-n) f.   *electrical outlet*
Die Steckdose ist links vom Schreibtisch.
The electrical outlet is to the left of the desk.

stehen   *to stand*
Die Gruppe steht in der vollen U-Bahn.
The group is standing in the packed subway.

Stein(-e) m.   *stone*
Wer im Glashaus sitzt, soll nicht mit Steinen werfen.
Those who sit in glass houses should not throw stones.

stellen   *to place*
Er stellt die Bücher ins Regal.
He places the books on the shelf.

Stellung(-en) f.   *position*
Sie hat die neue Stellung in der Firma bekommen.
She got the new position at the company.

Stempel m.   *stamp*
Bei der Einreise bekommen Sie einen Stempel in den Reisepass.
You get a stamp in your passport when you enter a country.

sterben   *to die*
Nach langer schwerer Krankheit ist er gestorben.
He died after a long, serious illness.

Steuer(-n) f.   *tax*
Die Steuern sind in der Schweiz niedriger als in Deutschland
und Österreich.
The taxes are lower in Switzerland than in Germany and Austria.

Stiefel m.   *boot*
Zum Reiten trägt er Stiefel.
He wears boots while horseback riding.

Stift(-e) m.   *pen*
Ich schreibe lieber mit einem Stift als mit einem Bleistift.
I prefer to write with a pen rather than with a pencil.

still   *quiet*
Die Kinder sind heute brav und still.
The children are well-behaved and quiet today.

Stimme(-n) f.   *voice*
Wegen der Erkältung ist ihre Stimme derzeit etwas heiser.
Because of her cold, her voice is currently a little hoarse.

stimmen   *to be right, to agree*
Ja, das stimmt absolut.
Yes, that is absolutely right.

stinken   *to stink*
Hier stinkt es nach Schimmelkäse.
Something stinks like blue cheese.

Stock(Stockwerke) m.   *floor*
Zwei Stockwerke über uns finden Sie das Büro von
    Dr. Winkler.
Dr. Winkler's office is two floors above us.

stolz   *proud*
Die Mutter ist ganz stolz auf ihren Sohn.
The mother is very proud of her son.

Stolz m.   *pride*
Zu viel Stolz kann eine Sünde sein.
Too much pride can be a sin.

stören   *to disturb*
Der Lärm der Nachbarn stört die Kinder beim Schlafen.
The neighbor's noise disturbs the children's sleep.

Störung(-en) f.   *disruption, malfunction*
Bitte melden Sie Störungen des Aufzugs beim Portier.
Please report any elevator malfunctions to the doorman.

S trafe(-n) f.   *penalty*
Die Strafe für falsches Parken beträgt 50 Euro.
The penalty for incorrect parking is 50 euros.

Strand(Strände) m.   *beach*
Auf Sylt gibt es so schöne Strände.
There are such nice beaches in Sylt.

Straße(-n) f.   *street*
Sie spaziert auf der Straße.
She is going for a walk on the street.

Straßenbahn(-en) f.   *Streetcar*
Mit der Straßenbahn kann man um die Wiener Innenstadt herum
    fahren.
You can take the streetcar in a loop around downtown Vienna.

Strauch(Sträucher) m.   *shrub*
In diesem Garten findet man schöne Sträucher.
There are pretty shrubs in this garden.

Strecke(-n) f.   *route*
Der LKW-fahrer fährt drei Mal die Woche die Strecke Berlin Mailand ab.
The truck driver drives the Berlin-Milan route three times a week.

strecken   *to stretch*
Jeden Morgen streckt sich Werner nachdem er aufsteht.
Every morning Werner stretches after he gets up.

streicheln   *to pet*
Ragenhild streichelt ihre Katze.
Ragenhild pets her cat.

streiten   *to quarrel*
Die zwei Kinder streiten über ein Spielzeug.
The two children quarrel over a toy.

Stress m.   *stress*
Jovanka hat diese Woche in der Arbeit sehr viel Stress.
Jovanka has a lot of stress at work this week.

stressig   *stressful*
Julianne ist glücklich, dass die stressige Prüfung vorbei ist.
Julianne is happy that the stressful exam is over.

Strich(-e) m.   *line*
Branko zieht einen Strich unter seine Unterschrift.
Branko draws a line under his signature.

stricken   *to knit*
Manuela strickt ihrem Mann einen Schal.
Manuela is knitting her husband a scarf.

Strom m.   *electricity*
Der Strom kommt aus der Steckdose in der Wand.
Electricity comes from the outlet on the wall.

Stromausfall m.   *power outage*
Wegen des Stromausfalls haben wir nicht fernsehen können.
Because of the power outage, we were not able to watch TV.

Stück(-e) n.   *piece*
Ich hätte gerne ein Stück Kuchen.
I would like a piece of cake.

Student(-en) m. **Studentin(-nen)** f.   *student (in college or university)*
Der Student arbeitet als Lehrassistent an der Universität.
The student works as a teaching assistant at the university.

Stuhl(Stühle) m.   *stool*
Sie sitzt auf einem Stuhl in der Küche.
She sits on a stool in the kitchen.

Sturm(Stürme) m.   *storm*
Die Stürme haben an der Küste großen Schaden verursacht.
The storms caused great damage to the coast.

suchen   *to search for*
Wir suchen nach einer fleißigen Person für diese Stelle.
We are looking for a hard-working person to fill this position.

Sucht(-en) f.   *addiction*
Sucht ist ein großes gesellschaftliches Problem.
Addiction is a major societal problem.

süchtig   *addicted*
Der junge Mann wird verhaftet, weil er leider auf Drogen süchtig ist.
The young man is being arrested because he is unfortunately addicted to drugs.

Süden m.   *south*
München liegt im Süden von Deutschland.
Munich is in the south of Germany.

Sünde(-n) f.   *sin*
Der Pastor erinnert die Gemeinde, keine Sünden zu begehen.
The pastor reminds the congregation not to commit any sins.

süß   *sweet, cute*
Wolfgang mag die Limonade nicht, weil er sie zu süß findet.
Wolfgang does not like the lemonade because he finds it too sweet.

Süßigkeit(-en) f.   *sweets*
Die Kinder essen natürlich gern Süßigkeiten.
Of course the children like to eat sweets.

Synagoge(-n) f.   *synagogue*
In der Synagoge versammeln sich viele für die Feiertage.
Many people gather in the synagogue for the holidays.

T

Tablett(-e) n.   *tray*
  Die Kellner in Wien servieren den Kaffee auf einem silbernen
    Tablett.
  Waiters in Vienna serve coffee on a silver tray.

Tablette(-n) f.   *pill*
  Der Patient beklagt sich, weil er so viele Tabletten schlucken
    muss.
  The patient complains because he has to swallow so many pills.

Tafel(-n) f.   *board*
  Die Lehrerin schreibt viel auf der Tafel und die Schüler schreiben
    alles in die Hefte.
  *The teacher writes a lot on the board and the students write it all in
    their notebooks.*

Tag(-e) m.   *day*
  Im Herbst warden die Tage kürzer.
  In fall the days get shorter.

tagen   *to meet*
  Die Politiker tagen in Stuttgart.
  The politicians are meeting in Stuttgart.

Tagung(-en) f.   *conference*
  Der Professor ist auf einer Tagung in Leipzig.
  The professor is at a conference in Leipzig.

tanken   *to fill a gas tank*
  Er tankt seinen Wagen mit Diesel.
  He fills his car's gas tank with diesel.

Tankstelle(-n) f.   *gas station*
  Bei der Tankstelle hat er den Luftdruck der Reifen geprüft.
  He checked his tire pressure at the gas station.

tanzen   *to dance*
  In Wien tanzt man gern Walzer.
  In Vienna, people like to waltz.

tapezieren   *to wallpaper*
  Der Vater tapeziert das Kinderzimmer.
  The father is wallpapering the children's room.

Tasche(-n) f.   *bag*
In seiner Tasche haben wir zwei Flaschen Wein gefunden.
We found two bottles of wine in his bag.

Taschenlampe(-n) f.   *flashlight*
Mit der Taschenlampe spaziert er nachts im Wald.
He walks through the forest at night with a flashlight.

Taschentuch(-tücher) n.   *tissue*
Weil ich erkältet bin, muss ich mir Taschentücher kaufen.
Because I have a cold, I need to buy some tissues.

Tasse(-n) f.   *cup*
Nach dem Abendessen trinkt er gern eine Tasse Earl Grey.
After dinner he likes to drink a cup of Earl Grey tea.

Tatsache(-n) f.   *fact*
Ihre Ausrede ändert nichts an der Tatsache, dass Sie zu spät sind.
Your excuse does not change anything about the fact that you're late.

tatsächlich   *actually*
Das ist tatsächlich eine interessante Geschichte.
This is actually an interesting story.

tauchen   *to dive*
Sie taucht gern im Meer und beobachtet die Fische.
She likes to dive in the ocean and watch the fish.

Taxi(-s) m.   *cab*
Er fährt mit dem Taxi zum Flughafen.
He takes a cab to the airport.

Teil(-e) m.   *part*
Sie hat das Stück Papier in zwei Teile zerrissen.
She tore the piece of paper into two parts.

teilnehmen   *to participate*
Er nimmt an der Veranstaltung teil.
He participates in the event.

Telefon(-e) n.   *phone*
Er spricht mit seiner Schwester auf dem Telefon.
He speaks with his sister on the phone.

telefonieren   *to phone, call*
Herr Müller telefoniert mit seinen Kindern.
Mr. Müller calls his children on the phone.

Teller m.   *plate*
Beim Buffet lädt er verschiedene schwedische Spezialitäten
auf seinen Teller.
*At the buffet table he puts assorted Swedish specialities on his
plate.*

Tennis spielen   *to play tennis*
Er spielt mit seinem Chef Tennis.
He is playing tennis with his boss.

Termin(-e) m.   *appointment*
Morgen habe ich einen Termin beim Arzt.
Tomorrow I have an appointment at the doctor's.

Terrorismus m.   *terrorism*
Der Terrorismus ist ein Problem in der Welt.
Terrorism is a problem in the world.

teuer   *expensive*
Die Preise in diesem Geschäft sind sehr teuer.
The prices in this store are very expensive.

Teufel m.   *devil*
Der Teufel schläft nie.
The devil never sleeps.

Theater n.   *theater*
Im Theater habe ich ein Stück von Goethe gesehen.
I saw a play by Goethe at the theater.

Thermometer n.   *thermometer*
Das Thermometer zeigt 25 Grad an.
The thermometer reads 25 degrees.

tief   *deep*
Er stecht tief in die Erde.
He digs deep in the soil.

Tiefgarage(-n) f.   *underground garage*
In vielen deutschen Städten findet man Tiefgaragen.
There are underground garages in many German cities.

Tisch(-e) m.   *table*
Salz und Pfeffer stehen auf dem Tisch.
Salt and pepper are on the table.

Tod(-e) m.   *death*
Nach dem Tod des Dichters haben viele um den großen
    Künstler getrauert.
After the death of the poet, many people mourned the great artist.

Toilette(-n) f.   *toilet, restroom*
Die Toilette befindet sich gleich nebenan vom Badezimmer.
The toilet is located directly next to the bathroom.

Topf(Töpfe) m.   *(kitchen) pot*
Im Topf kocht Markus ein würziges Gulasch.
Markus is cooking a spicy goulash in the pot.

Topflappen m.   *oven cloth/mit*
Sie hebt den heißen Topf mit einem Topflappen.
She lifts the hot pot with an oven mit.

Tor(-e) n.   *gate*
Das Tor zum Park war leider schon verschlossen.
Unfortunately, the park gate was already closed.

tot   *dead*
Das Wildschwein lag tot auf der Autobahn zwischen Magdeburg
    und Potsdam.
The wild boar lay dead on the highway between Magdeburg and Potsdam.

tragen   *to carry*
Sie trägt zwei Koffer zum Flughafen.
She is carrying two suitcases to the airport.

Traktor(-en) m.   *tractor*
Der Bauer fährt einen Traktor über das Feld.
The farmer drives a tractor across the field.

tratschen   *to gossip*
Die Kerle tratschen gern im Gasthaus.
The guys like to gossip at the inn.

Trauer f.   *sorrow*
Mit großer Trauer habe ich vom Ableben ihres Vaters gelesen.
I read about the passing of your father with great sorrow.

Traum(Träume) m.   *dream*
Das Mädchen hat große Träume für ihre Zukunft.
The girl has big dreams for her future.

träumen   *to dream*
Erich träumt in der Arbeit vom Urlaub.
Erich dreams of vacation while at work.

traurig   *sad*
Der Sohn ist sehr traurig über das Ableben des Vaters.
The son is very sad about the passing of his father.

treffen   *to meet*
Robert und Susanne treffen sich in einem Kaffeehaus.
Robert and Susanne are meeting at a café.

Treffpunkt(-e) m.   *meeting point*
Der Treffpunkt für unserer Abreise ist der Eingang zum
    Hauptbahnhof.
*The meeting point for our departure is the entry to the main
    railway station.*

Treppe(-n) f.   *staircase*
Die Treppe führt vom Erdgeschoß in den ersten Stock.
The staircase leads from the ground floor to the first floor.

treu   *faithful*
Johann ist seiner Frau immer treu.
Johann is always faithful to his wife.

Treue f.   *faithfulness*
Das Geschäft gibt seinen Kunden für deren Treue ein kleines
    Geschenk.
The store gives its customers a small gift for their faithfulness.

Trinkgeld(-gelder) n.   *tip*
In der Schweiz akzeptieren viele Kellner kein Trinkgeld.
In Switzerland, many waiters don't accept tips.

Triumph(-e) m.   *triumph*
Das gestrige Fussballspiel war ein weiterer Triumph für die
    Mannschaft.
Yesterday's soccer game was another triumph for the team.

trocken   *dry*
Nach dem vielen Regen ist es jetzt wieder trocken.
After all the rain, it is now dry again.

Trommel(-n) f.   *drum*
Der Junge schlägt auf die Trommel.
The boy beats the drum.

Trompete(-n) f.   *trumpet*
Markus spielt gern auf seiner Trompete.
Markus likes to play his trumpet.

Tuch(Tücher) n.   *towel*
Im Badezimmer findest du mehrere Tücher.
You will find several towels in the bathroom.

Tugend(-en) f.   *virtue*
Die Pünktlichkeit ist eine geschätzte Tugend.
Punctuality is an appreciated virtue.

tun   *to do*
In diesem Ort gibt es nicht viel zu tun.
There is not a lot to do in this town.

Tür(-en) f.   *door*
Mach bitte die Tür zu, denn es zieht.
Please close the door because there is a draft.

Türke(-n) m. **Türkin(-nen)** f.   *Turkish person*
Herr Özel ist Türke und kommt aus Ankara.
Mr. Özel is Turkish and comes from Ankara.

Türkei f.   *Turkey*
Die Türkei ist ein Land im Südosten von Europa.
Turkey is a country in Southeastern Europe.

türkisch   *Turkish*
Der türkische Kaffee schmeckt vielen Leuten besonders gut.
A lot of people like to flavor of Turkish coffee.

Türsteher m   *doorman*
Der Türsteher gewährt nur eingeladenen Gästen Zutritt
    zum Fest.
The doorman makes sure only invited guests get into the party.

Tüte(-n) f.   *shopping bag (in Germany only)*
Holger bringt zwei volle Tüten vom Supermarkt zurück.
*Holger brings two full shopping bags back from the grocery
    store.*

typisch   *typical*
Das ist typisch für Markus, dass er immer zu spät kommt.
It is typical of Markus to always arrives late.

U

U-Bahn(-en) f.   *subway*
Mit der U-Bahn fährt man schnell durch Hamburg.
You can travel through Hamburg quickly by subway.

über   *over*
Die Lampe hängt über dem Tisch.
The lamp hangs over the table.

überall   *everywhere*
Überall in Wien findet man leicht gute Mehlspeisen.
You can easily find good desserts everywhere in Vienna.

überfliegen   *to fly over*
Wenn wir nach Amerika fliegen, überfliegen wir manchmal
  Grönland.
When we fly to North America, we sometimes fly over Greenland.

überfluten   *to flood*
Die Donau hat mehrere Orte in der Wachau überflutet.
The Danube flooded several places in the Wachau region of Austria.

überleben   *to survive*
Nur wenige haben die Katasthrophe überlebt.
Only a few people survived the catastrophe.

übermorgen   *day after tomorrow*
Er hat übermorgen einen Termin beim Arzt.
He has an appointment with the doctor the day after tomorrow.

übernachten   *to spend the night*
Er übernachtet in einem Hotel.
He is spending the night in a hotel.

überqueren   *to cross*
Er überquert die Straße.
He crosses the street.

überreden   *to talk into*
Sie überredet ihre Familie den Urlaub in der Schweiz zu verbringen.
She talks her family into spending their vacation in Switzerland.

überzeugen   *to convince*
Der Verkäufer hat uns überzeugt, dass das rote Auto schöner
  ist als das blaue.
The salesperson convinced us that the red car was prettier than the blue one.

übrigens   *by the way*
Heute ist übrigens der letzte Tag im Semester.
By the way, today is the last day of the semester.

Uhr(-en) f.   *watch*
Sie hat sich eine neue Uhr gekauft.
She bought a new watch.

um   *at, around*
Wir kommen um 20 Uhr in Wien an.
We will arrive in Vienna at 8 pm.

Umfrage(-n) f.   *survey*
In dieser Umfrage wurden Konsumenten nach deren
   Lieblingsparfüm befragt.
In this survey, consumers were asked about their favorite perfume.

umkehren   *to turn around*
Das Flugzeug musste über dem Atlantik umkehren, weil ein
   Passagier erkrankt war.
*The airplane had to turn around over the Atlantic because a passenger
   had become sick.*

Umschlag(-schläge) f.   *envelope*
Er legt den Brief in einen Umschlag.
He puts the letter into an envelope.

Umstand(-stände) m.   *circumstance, fact*
Dieser Umstand beweist nicht das Verbrechen.
This circumstance does not prove the crime.

umziehen   *to relocate*
Die Firma zieht von Bonn nach Berlin um
The company is relocating from Bonn to Berlin.

Umzug(-züge) m.   *move*
Der Umzug von Augsburg nach Ulm ist gut verlaufen.
The move from Augsburg to Ulm went well.

unabhängig   *independent*
Wir lesen gerne unabhängige Zeitungen.
We like to read independent newspapers.

unbedingt   *unconditional, absolutely*
Wir müssen morgen unbedingt in die Apotheke.
We absolutely have to go to the pharmacy tomorrow.

unbekannt   *unknown*
Der Autor des Buches is unbekannt.
The author of the book is unknown.

unbequem   *uncomfortable*
Dieses Sofa ist leider sehr unbequem.
Unfortunately, this couch is very uncomfortable.

und   *and*
Ich möchte bitte einen Hamburger und Pommes Frites.
I would like a hamburger and fries.

undankbar   *ungrateful*
Der Junge war sehr undankbar für vielen Geschenke, die er zum
   Geburtstag bekommen hat.
*The boy was very ungrateful for the many presents he got for his
   birthday.*

Unfall(-fälle) m.   *accident*
Er hat einen schrecklichen Unfall gehabt und seitdem ist er
   gelähmt.
He had a terrible accident and since then has been paralyzed.

unfassbar   *incomprehensible*
Die Nachrichten des Unfalls sind unfassbar.
The news of the accident is incomprehensible.

ungefähr   *approximately*
Salzburg ist ungefähr 300 km von Wien entfernt.
Salzburg is approximately 300 kilometers from Vienna.

ungesund   *unhealthy*
Rauchen ist ungesund.
Smoking is unhealthy.

unglaublich   *unbelievable*
Die Geschichte, die mir der Nachbar erzählt hat, ist unglaublich.
The story that my neighbor told me is unbelievable.

Unglück n.   *misfortune, bad luck*
Die Familie hat ein großes Unglück befallen.
The family had a great misfortune.

unglücklich   *unhappy*
Sie ist sehr unglücklich über die vielen Veränderungen in der Stadt.
She is very unhappy about the many changes in the city.

unhöflich   *impolite*
Michael ist unhöflich, denn er grüßt seine Kollegen nicht.
Michael is impolite because he does not greet his colleagues.

Universität(-en) f.   *university, college*
Die Schweiz hat ausgezeichnete Universitäten.
Switzerland has excellent universities.

Unkraut(-kräuter) n.   *weed*
Die Unkräuter im Garten muss man jäten.
You need to pick the weeds in the garden.

unreif   *immature*
Dieses Kind ist noch sehr unreif.
This child is still very immature.

Unruhe(-n) f.   *unrest*
Die Unruhe im Krisengebiet hat sich verschlimmert.
The unrest in the crisis area has gotten worse.

unten   *down there*
Unten wartet ein Paket auf dich.
A package is waiting for you down there.

unter   *under*
Das Buch liegt unter dem Tisch.
The book is under the table.

unterdrücken   *oppress*
Der Diktator unterdrückt sein Volk.
The dictator oppresses his people.

Unterführung(-en) f.   *underground passage*
Wir benutzen die Unterführung, weil das sicherer ist.
We use the underground passage because it is safer.

unterhalten   *to entertain*
Der Zauberer unterhält die Kinder.
The magician entertains the children.

Unterhaltung(-en) f.   *entertainment*
Dieser Film sorgt für gute Unterhaltung.
This film makes for good entertainment.

Unterricht m.   *lesson*
Paul stört wieder den Unterricht durch lautes Schnarchen.
Paul disturbs the lesson again with his loud snoring.

unterrichten   *to teach*
Sie unterrichtet isländisch an der Universität.
She teaches Icelandic at the university.

Unterschied(-e) m.   *difference*
Der Unterschied zwischen einer Mücke und einem Elefanten
    ist enorm.
The difference between a mosquito and an elephant is enormous.

unterschiedlich   *different*
Bei dem Treffen hat er unterschiedlichen Menschen getroffen.
He met different kinds of people at the meeting.

unterschreiben   *to sign*
Morgen unterschreiben wir den Vertrag.
Tomorrow we will sign the contract.

unterstützen   *to support*
Er unterstützt seine Familie finanziell.
He supports his family financially.

Untertasse(-n) f.   *saucer*
Er gibt die Tasse zurück auf die Untertasse.
He puts the cup back on the saucer.

Unterwäsche(-n) f.   *underwear*
Er kauft sich neue Unterwäsche im Kaufhaus.
He is buying new underwear at the department store.

Unwetter n.   *bad weather*
Heute herrscht so ein Unwetter, dass wir zu Hause bleiben
    müssen.
There is such bad weather today that we have to stay at home.

unwichtig   *unimportant*
Das sind ja wirklich unwichtige Details, die mich nicht
    interessieren.
Those are really unimportant details that do not interest me.

unzufrieden   *dissatisfied*
Wir waren mit dem Service hier sehr unzufrieden.
We were really dissatisfied with the service here.

Urlaub(-e) m.   *vacation*
Familie Schabowski fährt dieses Jahr im Urlaub nach Neuseeland.
The Schabowski family is going on vacation in New Zealand this year.

Ursprung(-sprünge) m. *origin*
Der Ursprung dieser Torte findet sich in Budweis.
The origin of this torte is in the Czech city of Budweis.

Urteil(-e) n. *judgement*
Der Richter hat das Urteil verkündet.
The judge pronounced his judgement.

Urwald(-wälder) m. *jungle*
Er fährt in den Urwald in Brasilien.
He is traveling to the Brazilian jungle.

utopisch *utopian*
Das sind utopische Ideen, die unmöglich sind.
Those are impossible utopian ideas.

V

Vase(-n) f. *vase*
In der Vase stehen schöne rote Rosen von ihrem Freund.
There are pretty red roses from her boyfriend in the vase.

vegetarisch *vegetarian*
Ein vegetarisches Mahl enthält kein Fleisch.
A vegetarian meal contains no meat.

verändern *to change*
Wir haben die Speisekarte verändert und glauben, dass sie jetzt
besser ist.
We changed the menu and believe it to be better now.

Veränderung(-en) f. *change*
Er mag keine Veränderungen.
He does not like change.

Veranstaltung(-en) f. *event*
Das Museum bietet immer zahlreiche interessante
Veranstaltungen an.
The museum always offers numerous interesting events.

verantwortlich *responsible*
Der Direktor ist verantwortlich für die Schüler an dieser
Schule.
The principal is reponsible for the students at this school.

Verantwortung(-en) f.   *responsibility*
  Er trägt die Verantwortung für den Schaden, der bei diesem
    Unfall entstanden ist.
  He bears the responsibility for the damages caused by this accident.

verbessern   *to improve*
  Letztes Jahr wurden die Straßen in der Stadt verbessert.
  Last year the city streets were improved.

verbinden   *to connect*
  Die Autobahn A1 verbindet Salzburg mit Wien.
  The A1 highway connects Salzburg and Vienna.

verboten   *prohibited*
  Das Betreten der Geleise ist verboten.
  Stepping on the tracks is prohibited.

verbrauchen   *to use up*
  Wir sollten alle Lebensmittel in der Küche verbrauchen, bevor
    wir auf Urlaub gehen.
  *We should use up all groceries in the kitchen before we leave for
    vacation.*

Verbrechen n.   *crime*
  Das Verbrechen wurde von zwei Frauen verübt.
  The crime was perpetrated by two women.

Verbrecher m. **Verbrecherin(-nen)** f.   *criminal*
  Der Verbrecher sitzt schon seit mehreren Jahren im Gefängnis.
  The criminal has been sitting in prison for several years.

verbringen   *to spend*
  Er verbringt eine Woche in London.
  He is spending a week in London.

verdächtigen   *to suspect*
  Die Polizei verdächtigt den jungen Mann des Verbrechens.
  The police suspect the young man of committing the crime.

verdienen   *to earn*
  Sie verdient nicht viel mit ihrer Arbeit.
  She does not earn much with her work.

Verein m.   *club*
  Er ist dem Verein schon vor zwei Jahren beigetreten.
  He already joined the club two years ago

Verfassung(-en) f.   *constitution*
Deutschland hat keine Verfassung, sondern ein Grundgesetz.
Germany does not have a constitution, but rather a basic law.

verfehlen   *to miss*
Die Mannschaft hat ihr Ziel verfehlt.
The team missed its goal.

verfluchen   *to curse*
Die Hexe hat den Prinz verflucht.
The witch cursed the prince.

Vergangenheit(-en) f.   *past*
Die Schüler lernen in der Geschichteklasse über die
   Vergangenheit.
The students learn about the past in history class.

Vergangenheitsbewältigung(-en) f.   *coming to terms with the
   past*
Wegen der Geschichte des 20. Jahrhunderts ist die
   Vergangenheitsbewältigung ein großes Thema in der
   deutschen Gesellschaft.
*Coming to terms with the past is an important topic in German society
   because of twentieth-century history.*

vergeben   *to forgive*
So ein großes Verbrechen kann man nicht vergeben.
One cannot forgive such a significant crime.

vergessen   *to forget*
Es tut mir leid, aber ich habe die Tickets für das Konzert
   vergessen.
I am sorry, but I forgot the tickets for the concert.

vergleichen   *to compare*
Er vergleicht den einen Computer mit einem anderen.
He compares one computer with another.

vergnügen   *to have fun*
In einem Themenpark kann man sich schön vergnügen.
You can have a lot of fun at a theme park.

verkaufen   *to sell*
Uwe will sein altes Auto verkaufen.
Uwe wants to sell his old car.

Verkäufer m. **Verkäuferin(-nen)** f.   *seller*
Der Verkäufer erklärt dem Kunden wie der Drucker funktioniert.
The salesperson explains to the customer how the printer works.

Verkehr(-e) m.   *traffic*
Der Verkehr auf der A8 ist heute sehr stark.
The traffic on highway A8 is very heavy today.

Verlag(-e) m.   *publishing house*
Die größten deutschen Verlage befinden sich in Frankfurt.
The largest German publishing houses are located in Frankfurt.

verlassen   *to leave*
Wir verlassen Düsseldorf und ziehen nach Berlin um.
We are leaving Dusseldorf and moving to Berlin.

Verlassenschaft(-en) f.   *estate*
Der Notar ordnet die Verlassenschaft des Verstorbenen.
The notary is sorting out the deceased person's estate.

verlaufen   *to get lost*
Weil Sigrid ihre Karte im Hotel gelassen hat, hat sie sich in Rom
    verlaufen.
Because Sigrid left her map in the hotel, she got lost in Rome.

verletzen   *to injure*
Hilde ist vom Rad gefallen und hat sich dabei verletzt.
Hilde fell off her bike and injured herself.

verleugnen   *to deny*
Er verleugnet seine Verantwortung in diesem Fall.
He denies his responsibility in this case.

verlieren   *to lose*
Sie hat ihr Handy im Einkaufszentrum verloren.
She lost her cell phone at the mall.

verloben   *to become engaged*
Die zwei haben sich verlobt.
The two are engaged.

Verlobung(-en) f.   *engagement*
Das Paar feiert heute Verlobung.
The couple is celebrating their engagement today.

Verlust(-e) m.   *loss*
Der Verlust des Reisepasses muss bei der Polizei angezeigt werden.
The loss of a passport must be reported to the police

vermeiden   *to avoid*
Er vermeidet es, Alkohol zu trinken.
He avoids drinking alcohol.

Vermögen n.   *wealth*
Der Anwalt verwaltet das Vermögen der Familie.
The attorney manages the family's wealth.

vernichten   *to destroy*
Die Bombe hat das U-Boot vernichtet.
The bomb destroyed the submarine.

verpassen   *to miss*
Er hat die letzte U-Bahn des Tages verpasst.
He missed the last subway of the day.

verrückt   *crazy*
Unser Chef hat immer verrückte Ideen.
Our boss always has crazy ideas.

versammeln   *to gather*
Die Gruppe versammelt sich vor der Schule.
The group gathers in front of the school.

Versammlung(-en) f.   *meeting*
Leider hatte ich keine Zeit an der Versammlung teilzunehmen.
Unfortunately, I had no time to participate in the meeting.

verschmutzen   *to pollute*
Diese Fabrik verschmutzt die Umwelt.
This factory pollutes the environment.

verschwenden   *to waste*
Er verschwendet sein Geld für dumme Sachen.
He wastes his money on stupid things.

versichert   *insured*
Er ist gegen Diebstähle versichert.
He is insured against theft.

Versicherung(-en) f.   *insurance*
Ohne Versicherung darf man kein Auto lenken.
You may not operate a car without insurance.

versinken   *to sink*
Die Titanic ist nach einem Zusammenstoß mit einem Eisberg im Nordatlantik versunken.
The Titanic sank in the North Atlantic after crashing into an iceberg.

verspäten   *to delay*
Der Interregio-Express aus Rosenheim ist 25 Minuten verspätet.
The Interregio-Express train from Rosenheim is delayed by 25 minutes.

Verspätung(-en) f.   *delay*
Die Maschine aus Athen hat über eine Stunde Verspätung.
The plane from Athens has a delay of over an hour.

versprechen   *to promise*
Er verspricht ihm, das Geld zurückzuzahlen.
He promises to pay back the money.

Versprechen n.   *promise*
Er hält immer sein Versprechen.
He always keeps his promise.

Verstand m.   *intellect*
Herr Mayer hat den nötigen Verstand für diese komplizierte
   Arbeit.
Mr. Mayer has the necessary intellect for this complicated work.

verstecken   *to hide*
Die Kinder verstecken sich hinter dem Sofa, um den Vater zu
   überraschen.
The children are hiding behind the couch to surprise their father.

verstehen   *to understand*
Sie versteht 12 Sprachen relativ gut.
She understands twelve languages relatively well.

versuchen   *to try*
Er versucht, Deutsch zu lernen.
He is trying to learn German.

Vertrag(Verträge) m.   *contract*
Ich habe den Vertrag mit meinem neuen Arbeitgeber schon
   unterschrieben.
I have already signed the contract with my new employer.

vertragen   *to get along*
Die Kinder haben sich am Wochenende gut vertragen.
The children got along well over the weekend.

Vertrauen n.   *trust*
Er hat kein Vertrauen in die Politik.
He has no trust in politics.

verwalten   *to manage*
Der Notar verwaltet das Vermögen der Familie.
The notary manages the family's wealth.

verwenden   *to use*
Für den Kauf des iPhones verwendet er seine Kreditkarte.
He uses his credit card to buy the iPhone.

verwundern   *to amaze*
Er ist verwundert darüber, wie gut das kleine Mädchen singen
  kann.
He is amazed at how well the little girl can sing.

verzeihen   *to forgive*
Er hat ihr noch immer nicht verziehen.
He has still not forgiven her.

verzweifeln   *to despair*
Er verzweifelt an der traurigen Situation.
He despairs in the sad situation.

viel   *much*
Wir haben uns schon lang nicht mehr gesehen, also werden wir
  uns viel zu erzählen haben.
*We haven't seen each other for a long time, so we will have much to
  tell each other.*

Vielerlei pl.   *all sorts of*
Er sammelt vielerlei Briefmarken.
He collects all sorts of stamps.

vielleicht   *perhaps*
Vielleicht ist David schon mit der Arbeit fertig.
Perhaps David has already completed his work.

Viertel n.   *quarter*
Er trinkt ein Viertel Wein.
He is drinking a quarter (liter) of wine.

Vignette(-n) f.   *toll sticker*
Die Maut auf der Autobahn in Österreich und der Schweiz
  bezahlt mit einer auf dem Fenster angebrachten
  Vignette.
*The highway toll in Austria and Switzerland is paid with a toll sticker
  that you stick on the car window.*

Volk(Völker) n.   *people*
Das Volk winkt vor dem Schloss der Königin.
The people wave in front of the palace to the queen.

Volksschule(-n) f.   *elementary school*
Kinder im Alter von 6 bis 10 gehen in die Volksschule.
Children aged 6 to 10 attend elementary school.

voll   *full*
Er trägt ein volles Glas Milch ins Esszimmer.
He is carrying a full glass of milk into the dining room.

vor   *in front of*
Wir warten auf dich vor dem Theater.
We will wait for you in front of the theater.

vorbei   *over*
Das Konzert ist schon vorbei.
The concert is already over.

vorbeikommen   *to come by/over*
Die Eltern kommen morgen bei uns vorbei.
Our parents will come over to our house tomorrow.

vorbereiten   *to prepare*
Der Lehrer bereitet seine Stunde vor.
The teacher is preparing his lesson.

vorbeugen   *to prevent*
Um gegen Krankheiten vorzubeugen, bekommen Kinder
    Impfungen.
Children are given immunizations to prevent illnesses.

vorgestern   *day before yesterday*
Vorgestern sind wír nach Lübeck gefahren.
The day before yesterday we drove to Lübeck.

vorhaben   *to have in mind*
Für das Wochenende haben wir nichts vor.
We have nothing in mind for the weekend.

Vorhang(-hänge) m.   *curtain*
Sie hat sich für das Wohnzimmer neue Vorhänge gekauft.
She bought new curtains for her living room.

vorher   *beforehand*
Er hat vorher bei einer anderen Firma gearbeitet.
He worked for a different company beforehand.

Vorschau(-en) f.   *preview*
Im Kino habe ich eine Vorschau für einen neuen Film gesehen.
I saw a preview for a new movie at the movie theater.

vorsicht   *beware*
Vorsicht! Das Kabel steht unter Strom.
Beware! The electricity cable is live.

vorsichtig   *carefully*
Er öffnet vorsichtig die Flasche, denn er will nichts verschütten.
*He opens the bottle carefully because he doesn't want to spill
    anything.*

vorwärts   *forward*
Der Wagen fährt nur zwei Meter vorwärts.
The car only drives two meters forward.

Vulkan(-e) m.   *volcano*
In Island ist wieder ein Vulkan ausgebrochen.
A volcano in Iceland erupted again.

W

Waage(-n) f.   *scale*
Auf der Waage wird das Gewicht abgemessen.
Weight is measured on a scale.

wachsen   *to grow*
Die Sonnenblumen wachsen groß.
The sunflowers grow tall.

Wagen m.   *car*
Der Wagen ist kaputt und derzeit in der Werkstatt.
The car is broken and currently at the repair shop.

Wahl(-en) f.   *election*
Diese Partei hat die Wahl zum zweiten Mal gewonnen.
This party won the election for the second time.

wählen   *to vote*
Er wählt schon seit Jahren immer wieder die gleiche Partei.
He has been voting for the same party for years.

Wahnsinn(-e) m.   *insanity*
Diese Reise war ein Wahnsinn.
This trip was insanity.

wahr   *true*
Nein, das ist nicht wahr, sondern falsch.
No, that isn't true, it's false.

Wahrheit(-en) f.   *truth*
Jetzt haben wir die Wahrheit doch erfahren.
Now we learned the truth after all.

Währung(-en) f.   *currency*
Der Dollar ist die Währung der USA.
The dollar is the currency of the U.S.A.

Wald(Wälder) m.   *forest*
In Kärnten gibt es noch viele dicke Wälder.
There are still many dense forests in Carinthia.

wandern   *to hike*
Am Sonntag wird gewandert.
Sunday is a day for hiking.

Wanderung(-en) f.   *hike*
Wir haben am Sonntag eine schöne Wanderung durch den
    Schwarzwald gemacht.
We had a nice hike through the Black Forest on Sunday.

Ware(-n) f.   *goods, wares*
Die Waren in diesem Geschäft haben eine schlechte Qualität.
The goods in this store are of bad quality.

warm   *warm*
Im Sommer sind die Abende oft warm.
In summer the evenings are often warm.

Wärme f.   *warmth*
Er spürt die Wärme des Kachelofens.
He feels the warmth of the tiled stove.

warnen   *to warn*
Sie warnt die Menschen am Strand vor den Haien.
She warns the people on the beach about sharks.

warten   *to wait*
Er sitzt und wartet auf die Straßenbahn.
He is sitting and waiting for the streetcar.

Wärter m.   *guard*
Der Wärter bewacht nachts das Gebäude.
The guard watches over the building at night.

Warteraum(-räume) m.   *waiting room*
Im Warteraum ist das Rauchen strengstens verboten.
Smoking is strictly prohibited in the waiting room.

Warze(-n) f.   *wart*
Der Arzt entfernt dem Patienten eine Warze.
The doctor removes a wart from the patient.

Waschbecken n.   *sink*
Sie spült das Geschirr im Waschbecken.
She rinses the dishes in the sink.

waschen   *to wash*
Jeden Sonntag wäscht er seinen Wagen.
Every Sunday he washes his car.

Waschküche(-n) f.   *laundry room*
In der Waschküche haben wir eine Waschmaschine und einen
    Trockner.
We have a washing machine and a dryer in the laundry room.

Waschlappen m.   *washcloth*
Er putzt die Fenster mit einem Waschlappen.
He is cleaning the windows with a washcloth.

Waschmaschine(-n) f.   *washing machine*
Die Kleider werden in der Waschmaschine gewaschen.
The clothes are being washed in the washing machine.

Wasser n.   *water*
Das Wasser ist in diesem Bach sehr kalt.
The water in this stream is very cold.

Wasserhahn(-hähne) m.   *water tap*
Aus dem Wasserhahn kommt kein heißes Wasser.
There is no hot water coming out of the tap.

WC(-s) n.   *toilet, bathroom*
Das WC befindet sich am Ende des Gangs.
The bathroom is located at the end of the hallway.

Wecker m.   *alarm clock*
Der Wecker klingelt jeden Morgen um 6 Uhr.
The alarm clock goes off every morning at 6 am.

Weg(-e) m.   *way*
Können Sie mir den Weg nach Mariazell zeigen?
Can you show me the way to Mariazell?

Wegweiser m.   *signpost*
Auf dem Wegweiser steht, dass wir rechts abbiegen müssen.
The signpost says that we need to turn right.

weich   *soft*
Er schläft gern auf einer weichen Matratze.
He likes to sleep on a soft mattress.

Weihnachten n.   *Christmas*
Weihnachten ist ein wichtiger Feiertag im Christentum.
Christmas is an important holiday in Christianity.

Weihnachtsbaum(-bäume) m.   *Christmas tree*
Zu Weihnachten findet man in Deutschland viele
    Weihnachtsbäume.
*You will find many Christmas trees in Germany during the Christmas
    season.*

weil   *because*
Ich bin heute sehr müde, weil ich gestern nicht geschlafen habe.
I am very tired today because I did not sleep yesterday.

weinen   *to cry*
Wenn ich Zwiebeln schneide, muss ich immer weinen.
When I chop onions, I always have to cry.

weit   *far*
Er arbeitet weit weg von seiner Familie.
He works far away from his family.

Welle(-n) f.   *wave*
Die Wellen am Strand waren unglaublich hoch.
The waves on the beach were unbelievably high.

Welt(-en) f.   *world*
Er ist mit dem größten Passagierflugzeug der Welt geflogen.
He flew on the world's biggest passenger airplane.

wenden   *to turn around*
Ich glaube wir sind falsch gefahren, also werde ich den Wagen
    wenden.
I think that we went the wrong way, so I will turn the car around.

Wendung(-en) f.   *turn around*
Diese Geschichte hat am Ende eine interessante Wendung
    genommen.
This story took an interesting turn at the end.

Werbung(-en) f. *commercial*
Werbungen sind im öffentlich-rechtlichen Fernsehen nach
20 Uhr verboten.
Commercials are prohibited on public television after 8 pm.

werden *to become*
Uschi will Friseurin werden.
Uschi wants to become a hairdresser.

werfen *to throw*
Der Vater wirft seinem Sohn den Ball.
The father throws the ball to his son.

Werk(-e) n. *oeuvre, work, piece*
Das ist das beste Werk des Künstlers.
This is the artist's best oeuvre.

Werkzeug(-e) n. *tool*
Hast du die nötigen Werkzeuge für das Projekt?
Do you have the necessary tools for the project?

Wert(-e) m. *value*
Diese Briefmarken haben ihren Wert verloren.
These postage stamps have lost their value.

wesentlich *essential*
Dieses Auto ist wesentlich anders als das andere.
This car is essentially different than the other one.

Westen m. *west*
Rheinland-Pfalz ist eine Bundesland im Westen von
Deutschland.
Rhineland-Pallatine is a state in the west of Germany.

Wettbewerb(-e) m. *competition*
In diesem Wettbewerb werden wir erfahren, wer den besten
Apfelstrudel backen kann.
This competition will decide who can bake the best apple strudel.

Wette(-n) f. *bet*
Er ist ganz glücklich, denn er hat die Wette gewonnen.
He is very happy because he won the bet.

wetten *to bet*
Er wettet gern auf Pferde.
He likes to bet on horses.

Wetter n.   *weather*
Wie wird denn morgen das Wetter?
What will the weather be like tomorrow?

wichtig   *important*
Wenn man die Straße überquert, ist es wichtig, dass man nach
  rechts und links schaut.
It is important to look right and and left when crossing the street.

wickeln   *to wrap*
Er wickelt die Vase in ein großes Stück Papier.
He wraps the vase in a large piece of paper.

Widerstand(-stände) m.   *resistance*
Leider haben nur wenige Deutsche Widerstand gegen die Nazis
  geleistet.
*Unfortunately, few Germans were involved in the resistance against the
  Nazis.*

widerstehen   *to resist*
Der Schweizer Schokolade kann ich einfach nicht widerstehen.
I simply cannot resist Swiss chocolate.

wie   *how*
Sie versteht nicht wie Flugzeuge fliegen können.
She does not understand how airplanes can fly.

wieder   *again*
Warum erzählst du mir wieder den gleichen Witz?
Why are you telling me the same joke again?

wiederholen   *to repeat*
Der Lehrer wiederholt den Satz für die Schüler.
The teacher repeats the sentence for the students.

Wiederholung(-en) f.   *repetition, rerun*
Jetzt habe ich die Wiederholung des Fußballspiels verpasst.
Now I missed the rerun of the soccer game.

Wiege(-n) f.   *cradle*
Das Baby schläft in der Wiege.
The baby is sleeping in the cradle.

Wiese(-n) f.   *meadow*
Die zwei Damen pflücken Blumen auf der Wiese.
The two ladies are picking flowers in the meadow.

wild   *wild*
Rehe sind wilde Tiere.
Deer are wild animals.

Wille(-n) m.   *will*
Er bekommt immer was er will, weil er einen starken
   Willen hat.
He always gets what he wants because he has a strong will.

willkommen   *welcome*
Herzlich Willkommen, Frau Gruber!
A warm welcome to Ms. Gruber!

Wind(-e) m.   *wind*
Der Wind kann an der Nordseeküste ganz stark wehen.
The wind can blow very strong on the North Sea coast.

Windel(-n) f.   *diaper*
Bei Kleinkindern ist es wichtig, die Windeln regelmäßig zu
   wechseln.
It is important to regularly change babies' diapers.

winken   *to wave*
Die Königin winkt von ihrem Wagen aus zu den Bürgern auf
   der Straße.
The queen waves from her car to the citizens on the street.

wirken   *to work*
Dieses Medikament wirkt wirklich.
This medication really works.

wirklich   *really*
Er hatte wirklich keine Ahnung von dem Unfall.
He really had no idea of the accident.

Wirtschaft(-en) f.   *economy*
Die österreichische Wirtschaft hat sich durch Exporte nach
   Osteuropa gestärkt.
*The Austrian economy has been strengthened through exports to
   Eastern Europe.*

wissen   *to know*
Wir wissen leider noch immer nur wenig über die Krankheit.
We still only know a little about the disease.

Wissenschaft(-en) f.   *science*
Die Germanistik ist eine Wissenschaft, die die deutschsprachige
   Literatur untersucht.
Germanistics is a science that examines German-language literature.

Witwe(-n) f.   *widow*
Die Witwe lebt mit ihren vier Kindern in einem Haus in
   Hollabrunn.
The widow lives with her four children in a house in Hollabrunn.

Witwer m.   *widower*
Der arme Witwer trauert noch um seine liebe Frau.
The poor widower still mourns his dear wife.

Witz(-e) m.   *joke*
Gerhard erzählt die lustigsten Witze, über die ich immer lachen
   muss.
Gerhard tells the funniest jokes that always make me laugh.

witzig   *humorous*
Der witzige Schauspieler hat das Publikum gut unterhalten.
The humorous actor was good at entertaining the audience.

wohl   *probably*
Das ist wohl der höchste Baum, denn ich jemals gesehen habe.
This is probably the tallest tree that I have ever seen.

wohnen   *to live, to reside*
Frau Dubcek wohnt in einer Villa in Pressburg.
Ms. Dubcek lives in a villa in Bratislava.

Wohngemeinschaft(-en) f.   *shared living, shared apartment*
Ulrike lebt mit drei anderen Leuten in einer Wohngemeinschaft.
Ulrike lives with three other people in a shared apartment.

Wohnung(-en) f.   *apartment*
Otto hat eine schöne große Wohnung in Berlin.
Otto has a nice big apartment in Berlin.

Wohnzimmer n.   *living room*
Im Wohnzimmer steht unser altes Sofa und der Fernseher.
Our old couch and TV set are in the living room.

Wolke(-n) f.   *cloud*
Heute gibt es wieder viele Wolken im Himmel.
There are a lot of clouds in the sky again today.

Wolle f.   *wool*
Mein schöner roter Pullover ist aus Wolle.
My nice red sweater is made of wool.

wollen   *to want to*
Wir wollen zu Weihnachten der Kälte entkommen und Urlaub in Sri Lanka machen.
We want to escape the cold at Christmas and take a vacation in Sri Lanka.

Wort(-e) n.   *word*
Er ist sprachlos und ihm fehlen die Worte.
He is speechless and can't find the words.

Wörterbuch(-bücher) n.   *dictionary*
Wenn man ein Wort nicht kennt, muss man es im Wörterbuch nachschlagen.
If you don't know a word, you need to look it up in a dictionary.

Wunde(-n) f.   *wound*
Er geht zum Arzt, weil seine Wunde nur langsam heilt.
He goes to the doctor beceause his wound is healing slowly.

Wunder n.   *miracle*
Manchmal geschehen noch Wunder.
Sometimes miracles do happen.

wunderbar   *wonderful*
Er hat ein wunderbares Lied gesungen.
He sung a wonderful song.

wundern   *to be amazed*
Er wundert sich wie viel sich in der Stadt verändert hat.
He is amazed at how much has changed in the city.

Wunsch(Wünsche) m.   *wish*
Sie ist sehr bescheiden und hat keine Wünsche für Weihnachten.
She is very modest and has no wishes for Christmas.

wünschen   *to wish*
Das Mädchen wünscht sich eine Puppe zum Geburtstag.
The little girl is wishing for a doll for her birthday.

Würfel m.   *dice*
Die Würfel sind gefallen.
The dice have been rolled.

Wurzel(-n) f.   *root*
Wir haben in Berlin Wurzeln geschlagen.
We have put down roots in Berlin.

Wüste(-n) f.   *desert*
In der Wüste ist das Wasser ein kostbarer Schatz.
Water is a precious treasure in the desert.

Wut f.   *anger*
Er hat eine Wut auf die Terroristen, die so viele Menschen
ermordet haben.
He has anger for the terrorists who murdered so many people.

wütend   *angry*
Franz ist wütend über den Lärm, den die Nachbarn mit ihrer
lauten Musik verursachen.
Franz is angry about the noise from the neighbors' loud music.

Z

zahlen   *to pay*
Wir zahlen für das Essen im Restaurant.
We pay for the food at the restaurant.

zahlreich   *numerous*
Zahlreich Gäste sind zu der Feier erschienen.
Numerous guests came to the celebration.

Zahnbürste(-n) f.   *toothbrush*
Die Kinder putzen sich die Zähne mit einer Zahnbürste.
The children brush their teeth with a toothbrush.

Zahnpasta f.   *toothpaste*
Die Zahnpasta braucht man zum Zähne putzen.
You need toothpaste to brush your teeth.

Zauberei(-en) f.   *magic*
Magda ist abergläubisch und glaubt an Zauberei.
Magda is superstitious and believes in magic.

Zauberer m.   *magician*
Der Zauberer gibt eine Vorstellung.
The magician is giving a performance.

Zeichen n.   *symbol*
Im Krieg ist eine weiße Fahne ein Zeichen für Waffenstillstand.
During war, a white flag is a symbol for a ceasefire.

Zeichentrickfilm(-e) m. *Cartoon, animated film*
Die Deutschen sehen gern amerikanische Zeichentrickfilme.
The Germans like to watch American animated films.

zeichnen *to draw*
Der Künstler zeichnet ein Bild von der Dame.
The artist draws a picture of the lady.

Zeichnung(-en) f. *drawing*
Die Zeichnung des Künstlers gefällt uns sehr.
We really like the artist's drawing.

zeigen *to show*
Herr Nemet zeigt uns seine Briefmarkensammlung.
Mr. Nemet shows us his stamp collection.

Zeitschrift(-en) f. *magazine*
Beim Friseur lesen die Kunden gern Zeitschriften.
Customers like to read magazines at the hair salon.

Zeitung(-en) f. *newspaper*
Ich habe in der Zeitung gelesen, dass morgen die Ausstellung im
Museum eröffnet wird.
I read in the newspaper that the museum exhibition opens tomorrow.

Zentrum(Zentren) n. *center*
Im Zentrum der Stadt steht ein großes Einkaufszentrum.
There is a large mall in the city center.

zerreißen *to tear apart*
Er hat den Vertrag zerrissen.
He tore apart the contract.

zerstören *to destroy*
Die Fliegerbomben haben die Stadt im 2. Weltkrieg zerstört.
The air raid bombs destroyed the city in World War II.

Zettel(-n) m. *note, paper*
Er schreibt die Informationen auf einen Zettel.
He writes the information on a piece of paper.

Zeug(-e) n. *stuff*
Dieses Zeug mag ich nicht besonders.
I don't particularly like this stuff.

Zeuge(-n) m. **Zeugin(-nen)** f. *witness*
Das Gericht hat ihn als Zeugen zur Verhandlung eingeladen.
The court invited him to be a witness at the trial.

Zeugnis(-se) n.   *report card*
Am Ende des Schuljahres bekommen alle Schüler und
  Schülerinnen ein Zeugnis.
At the end of the school year, all students get a report card.

Ziegelstein(-e) m.   *brick*
Das rote Hause ist aus Ziegelstein.
The red house is made of brick.

ziehen   *to pull*
Er zieht einen kleinen Wagen die Straße entlang.
He pulls a small cart down the street.

Ziel(-e) n.   *goal*
Es ist das Ziel unserer Arbeit, Menschen zu helfen.
The goal of our work is to help people.

Zielgerade(-n) f.   *finish line*
Der Läufer hat die Zielgerade erreicht.
The runner reached the finish line.

Zielpunkt(-e) m.   *target*
Wilhelm Tell hat seinen Zielpunkt, den Apfel am Kopf seines
  Sohnes, getroffen.
William Tell hit his target, which was the apple on top of his son's head.

Zigarette(-n) f.   *cigarette*
Das Rauchen von Zigaretten schädigt die Gesundheit.
Cigarette smoking harms your health.

Zigarre(-n) f.   *cigar*
Manche Deutsche bringen Zigarren mit aus ihrem Urlaub
  auf Kuba.
Some Germans bring back cigars from their Cuban vacation.

Zimmer n.   *room*
Diese Wohnung hat große Zimmer mit Blick auf den Dom.
This apartment has large rooms with a view of the cathedral.

zittern   *to shiver*
Die Kinder zittern vor Kälte.
The children are shivering because of the cold.

Zoll(Zölle) m.   *customs*
Der Zoll kontrolliert die Koffer an der Grenze.
Customs checks suitcases at the border.

zu   *to*
Der Sohn bringt das Buch zu seiner Mutter.
The son brings the book to his mother.

zufrieden   *satisfied*
Der Chef ist mit der Arbeit seiner Angestellten sehr zufrieden
The boss is very pleased with his employees' work.

Zug(Züge) m.   *train*
Der Zug ist am Hauptbahnhof angekommen.
The train arrived at the main railroad station.

zuhören   *to listen*
Für Eltern ist es wichtig, dass sie ihren Kindern zuhören.
It is important for parents to listen to their children.

zulassen   *to permit*
Der Vater hat es nicht zugelassen, dass seine Tochter bis nach
  Mitternacht aus bleibt.
The father did not allow his daughter to stay out past midnight.

zulässig   *permissible*
Das Betreten dieses Zimmers ist nicht zulässig.
Entering this room is not permissible.

zurück   *back*
Nach dem Urlaub fahren wir wieder zurück nach Hause.
After the vacation, we drove back home again.

zurückhalten   *to hold back*
Peter hat sich im Streit mit seinem Kollegen nicht
  zurückgehalten.
Peter did not hold back in the argument with his colleague.

zusammen   *together*
Wir haben zusammen das Problem gelöst.
We solved the problem together.

Zustand(-stände) m.   *condition*
Das Haus war in einem schrecklichen Zustand und daher
  konnten wir es nicht kaufen.
The house was in terrible condition and that is why we could not buy it.

zustellen   *to deliver*
Der Briefträger hat mir einen wichtigen Brief zugestellt.
The mailman delivered an important letter to me.

Zwerg(-e) m.   *dwarf*

Schneewittchen war hinter den Bergen bei den sieben Zwergen.
Snow White was with the seven dwarfs behind the mountains.

zwicken   *to pinch*

Die Großmutter zwickt die Backen ihres Enkels.
The grandmother pinches her grandchild's cheeks.

Zwirn(-e) m.   *thread*

Er flickt seine Socken mit einem Stück Zwirn.
He mends his socks with a piece of thread.

zwischen   *between*

Der Außenminister sitzt zwischen dem Kanzler und dem
Präsidenten.
*The minister of foreign affairs is sitting between the chancellor and the
president.*

Category Section

Begrüßungen	Greetings
Adee!	Bye! (informally in Switzerland and southwestern Germany)
Auf Wiedersehen!	Goodbye!
Ba-ba!	Bye! (informally in Austria)
Ciao!	Bye! (informal)
Grüß Gott!	Hello! (in Austria and Southern Germany)
Grüezi!	Hello! (in Switzerland)
Guten Abend!	Good evening!
Guten Morgen!	Good morning!
Gute Nacht!	Good night!
Guten Tag!	Hello! (most common version)
Hallo!	Hello! (on the phone, or informally in Germany)
Servus!	Hello and Bye! (informally in Austria)
Tschüss!	Bye! (informally in Germany)

Berufe	Occupations
Architekt m.	architect
Arzt m.	physician
Bäcker m	baker
Bauer m.	farmer
Beamter m.	bureaucrat
Briefträger m.	letter carrier
Buchhalter m.	accountant
Buchhändler m.	bookseller

Dichter m.	poet
Fleischhauer m.	butcher
Flugbegleiter m.	flight attendant
Förster m.	forester
Friseur m.	hairdresser
Imam m.	iman
Installateur m.	plumber
Kaufmann m.	businessman
Kellner m.	waiter
Koch m.	cook
Konditor m.	pastry chef
Krankenpfleger m.	nurse
Lehrer m.	teacher
Musikant m.	musician
Notar m.	notary
Optiker m.	optometrist
Pfarrer m.	pastor
Pilot m.	pilot
Priester m.	priest
Professor m.	professor
Rabbiner m.	rabbi
Rechtsanwalt m.	attorney
Reporter m.	journalist
Sänger m.	singer
Schaffner m.	conductor
Schauspieler m.	actor
Schriftsteller m.	writer
Tänzer m.	dancer
Tierarzt m.	veterinarian

Essen und Trinken   **Food and Drink**

Backwaren   *Baked goods*

Berliner m.	jelly donut
Brezel f.	pretzel

Brot n.	bread
Brötchen n.	bread roll
Gugelhupf m.	bundt cake
Hörnchen n.	croissant
Kipferl n.	croissant
Krapfen m.	jelly donut
Kuchen m.	cake
Plunder m.	pastry
Roulade f.	jelly roll
Semmel f.	bread roll
Strudel m.	strudel
Torte f.	torte

Fleisch und Fisch	*Meat and Fish*
Aufschnitt m.	cold cuts
Braten m.	roast
Dorsch m.	cod
Ente f.	duck
Faschiertes n.	ground meat
Forelle f.	trout
Gans f.	goose
Garnele f.	shrimp
Huhn n.	chicken
Kalb n.	veal
Karpfen m.	carp
Kottelet n.	cutlet
Lachs m.	salmon
Laibchen n.	meatball
Lamm n.	lamb
Leber f.	liver
Leberkäse m.	liver cheese
Pangasius m.	pangasius catfish
Pastete f.	paté

Pferd n.	horse
Pute f.	turkey
Reh n.	venison
Rind n.	beef
Sardelle f.	anchovy
Schinken m.	ham
Schnitzel n.	schnitzel (breaded cutlet)
Schwein n.	pork
Stelze f.	shank
Thunfisch m.	tuna
Wild n.	game
Wildschwein n.	wild boar
Wurst f.	sausage

Milch und Eier — *Eggs and Dairy*

Butter f.	butter
Ei n.	egg
Eidotter m.	egg yolk
Eis n.	ice cream
Joghurt m.	yogurt
Käse m.	cheese
Kakao m.	chocolate (milk)
Margarine f.	margarine
Molke f.	whey drink
Rahm m.	cream
Rührei n.	scrambled egg
Schafskäse m.	sheep cheese
Schlagobers m.	whipped cream
Spiegelei n.	sunny side up egg
Streichkäse m.	cheese spread

Obst und Gemüse — *Fruit and Vegetables*

Apfel m.	apple
Birne f.	pear

Brokkoli m.	broccoli
Brombeere f.	blackberry
Erbse f.	pea
Erdbeere f.	strawberry
Gurke f.	cucumber
Heidelbeere f.	blueberry
Himbeere f.	raspberry
Karfiol m.	cauliflower
Karotte f.	carrot
Kartoffel f.	potato
Kirsche f.	cherry
Knoblauch m.	garlic
Marille f.	apricot
Melanzani f.	eggplant
Melone f.	melon
Olive f.	olive
Orange f.	orange
Paprika m.	pepper
Pilz m.	mushroom
Ribisel m.	currant
Salat m.	salad
Spargel m.	asparagus
Spinat m.	spinach
Stangensellerie m.	celery
Tomate f.	tomato
Traube f.	grape
Zitrone f.	lemon
Zwetschke f.	plum
Zwiebel f.	onion

Andere   *Other Items*

Brösel m.	bread crumb
Essig m.	vinegar

Honig m.	honey
Mehl n.	flour
Öl n.	oil
Pfeffer m.	pepper
Reis m.	rice
Salz n.	salt
Schokolade f.	chocolate
Senf m.	mustard
Zucker m.	sugar

Getränke / *Drinks*

Bier n.	beer
Cola f.	coke
Kaffee m.	coffee
Likör m.	liqueur
Limonade f.	lemonade, soda
Most m.	cider
Saft m.	juice
Schorle f.	sparkling juice
Sekt m.	champagne
Tee m.	tea
Wein m.	wine

Familie / Family

Bruder m.	brother
Cousin m.	male cousin
Eltern pl.	parents
Großmutter f.	grandmother
Großvater m.	grandfather
Kusine f.	female cousin
Mutter f.	mother
Onkel m.	uncle
Schwager m.	brother-in-law

Schwägerin f.	sister-in-law
Schwester f.	sister
Schwiegereltern pl.	in-laws
Schwiegermutter f.	mother-in-law
Schwiegervater m.	father-in-law
Sohn m.	son
Tante f.	aunt
Tochter f.	daughter
Urgroßmutter f.	great grandmother
Urgroßvater m.	great grandfather
Vater m.	father

Farben — Colors

blau	blue
braun	brown
gelb	yellow
grau	grey
grün	green
orange	orange
rosa	pink
rot	red
schwarz	black
silber	silver
violett	violet
weiß	white

Fragen — Questions

Warum machen wir das?	Why are we doing this?
Wer ist das?	Who is that?
Wie geht es Ihnen?	How are you?
Wie heißen Sie?	What is your name?
Wie spät is es?	What time is it?
Wo finde ich…?	Where do I find…?

Geschäfte

Apotheke f.	pharmacy
Bäckerei f.	bakery
Drogerie f.	drugstore
Einkaufszentrum n.	shopping mall
Fleischhauerei f.	butcher shop
Kaufhaus n.	department store
Schuhgeschäft n.	shoe store
Supermarkt m.	supermarket
Tabakladen m.	tobacco shop (in Germany)
Tabak-Trafik f.	tobacco shop (in Austria)
Zeitungskiosk m.	newsstand

Stores

Internet und Computer

Computer m.	computer
Browser m.	browser
Datei f.	file
Device n.	device (cell phones, iPods)
Drucker m.	printer
Handy n.	cell phone
herunterladen	to download
Internet n.	Internet
iPod m.	iPod
iPhone n.	iPhone
Laptop m.	laptop
Mail n.	e-mail
Maus f.	mouse
MP3-Spieler m.	MP3 player
Passwort n.	password
SMS f.	text message
USB Stick m.	flash drive
Videospiel n.	video game
WLAN n.	Wi-Fi

Internet and Computers

Jahreszeiten

Frühling m.

Herbst m.

Sommer m.

Winter m.

Kleidung

Anzug m.

Bluse f.

Hemd n.

Hose f.

Krawatte f.

Pullover m.

Pyjama n.

Rock m.

Schuh m.

Socken m.

Stiefel f.

Unterwäsche f.

Kommunikation und Medien

Abonnement n.

CD-Spieler m.

DVD-Spieler m.

Fernsehen n.

Fernseher m.

Kabelfernsehen n.

Kanal m.

Medien pl.

Nachrichten pl.

Radio n.

Sendung f.

Seasons

spring

fall

summer

winter

Clothing

suit

blouse

shirt

pants

tie

sweater

pajamas

skirt

shoe

socks

boots

underwear

Communication and Media

subscription

CD player

DVD player

TV

TV set

cable TV

channel

media

news

radio

program

Werbung f.	advertisement
Zeitschrift f.	magazine
Zeitung f.	newspaper

Körper	**Body**
Auge n.	eye
Arm m.	arm
Bauch m.	stomach
Bein n.	leg
Ellbogen m.	elbow
Finger m.	finger
Fuß m.	foot
Haar n.	hair
Hals m.	neck
Hand f.	hand
Knie n.	knee
Kopf m.	head
Mund m.	mouth
Nase f.	nose
Ohr n.	ear
Zehe f.	toe

Monate	**Months**
Januar m.	January
Februar m.	February
März m.	March
April m.	April
Mai m.	May
Juni m.	June
Juli m.	July
August m.	August
September m.	September

Oktober m.	October
November m.	November
Dezember m.	December

Notfälle | **Emergencies**

Ambulanz f.	ambulance
Feuerwehr f.	fire department
Notarzt m.	emergency physician
Polizei f.	police

Nummern | **Numbers**

null	0
eins	1
zwei	2
drei	3
vier	4
fünf	5
sechs	6
sieben	7
acht	8
neun	9
zehn	10
elf	11
zwölf	12
dreizehn	13
vierzehn	14
fünfzehn	15
zwanzig	20
einundzwanzig	21
zweiundzwanzig	22
dreißig	30
einunddreißig	31
vierzig	40

fünfzig	50
sechzig	60
siebzig	70
achtzig	80
neunzig	90
hundert	100
hunderteins	101
hundertzehn	110
hundertzweiundzwanzig	120
zweihundert	200
dreihundert	300
tausend	1,000
zweitausend	2,000

Tage	Days
Montag m.	Monday
Dienstag m.	Tuesday
Mittwoch m.	Wednesday
Donnerstag m.	Thursday
Freitag m.	Friday
Samstag m.	Saturday
Sonntag m.	Sunday

Tiere	Animals
Adler m.	eagle
Affe m.	monkey
Bär m.	bear
Frosch m.	frog
Fuchs m.	fox
Hund m.	dog
Katze f.	cat
Kuh f.	cow

Löwe m.	lion
Maus f.	mouse
Papagei m.	parrot
Pferd n.	horse
Schaf n.	sheep
Schildkröte f.	turtle
Schlange f.	snake
Taube f.	pigeon
Tiger m.	tiger
Wolf m.	wolf
Vogel m.	bird
Ziege f.	goat

Zeit   Time

Jahr n.	year
Minute f.	minute
Monat m.	month
Sekunde f.	second
Stunde f.	hour
Tag m.	day
Woche f.	week

German and English Cognates

German and English are Germanic languages. The majority of basic English high-frequency words are of Anglo-Saxon origin and therefore similar to German. There are many words in English with Norman (French) and Scandinavian origins, but quite a few of these words also exist in German. Some cognates are almost identical in both languages, while others are similar but have different spellings. In addition, there are words that do not appear related at first glance, but their connection becomes apparent after they are examined more closely. Identifying these cognates accelerates German vocabulary building for Anglophones.

1. Words that are (almost) identical in German and English:

Arm	*arm*
Auto	*auto*
Ball	*ball*
bitter	*bitter*
bringen	*to bring*
Bus	*bus*
Finger	*finger*
Gel	*gel*
Glas	*glass*
Gold	*gold*
Hand	*hand*
hängen	*to hang*
Information	*information*
Jupiter	*jupiter*
Musik	*music*
Ring	*ring*
Sand	*sand*
Sack	*sack, bag*
Saturn	*saturn*
singen	*to sing*

Sofa	*sofa*
Thermometer	*thermometer*
waschen	*to wash*
Wolf	*wolf*
Wolle	*wool*
Wunder	*wonder, miracle*
Wind	*wind*

2. Words that are similar, but spelled differently:

Banane	*banana*
halten	*to hold*
Haus	*house*
Kamera	*camera*
Kabel	*cable*
kalt	*cold*
Karte	*card*
Lippe	*lip*
Magazin	*magazine*
Maus	*mouse*
Medizin	*medicine*
Metall	*metal*
Nase	*nose*
Platik	*plastic*
Sandalen	*sandals*
sauer	*sour*
Schuh	*shoe*
Tabak	*tobacco*
tanzen	*to dance*
Theater	*theater*
Tomate	*tomato*
unter	*under*
Wunde	*wound*

3. Words that are related but not immediately apparent as such:

alt	*old*
Apfel	*apple*
besser	*better*
Bett	*bed*
Brot	*bread*
Buch	*book*
das	*that*
Eis	*ice*

Feuer	*fire*
Frucht	*fruit*
Fuß	*foot*
Gitarre	*guitar*
gut	*good*
Haar	*hair*
Heu	*hay*
Kuh	*cow*
Kupfer	*copper*
Nagel	*nail*
neu	*new*
Ohr	*ear*
Öl	*oil*
Parfüm	*perfume*
Pfanne	*pan*
Pfeffer	*pepper*
Pfennig	*penny*
Pflanze	*plant*
Salz	*salt*
sie	*she*
Silber	*silver*
Stahl	*steel*
stehlen	*to steal*
Stuhl	*stool, chair*
trinken	*drink*
Wasser	*water*

German Grammar Primer

Subject Pronouns

Singular	Plural
ich (I)	wir (we)
du (you—informal sing.)	ihr (you—informal pl.)
er (he)	sie (they); Sie (you—informal sing. and pl.)
sie (she)	
es (it)	

Note: You will hear German speakers use "man" (conjugated like "er, sie, es") instead of "du," "wir," or "Sie." German speakers prefer the impersonal "man" (English *one*) over the direct pronouns, which are perceived as being too imposing in general situations.

The informal "you" in German is "du" in the singular and "ihr" in the plural. It is only used with close friends and family, as well as with children and among students and soldiers. The formal "Sie" is conjugated like the third person plural "sie" and should be used as the default "you" for anyone learning German.

Regular verb formation

In German, the majority of verbs in the present tense are regular verbs. There are also stem-vowel changing verbs as well as irregular helping verbs.

kommen: to come

ich komm**e** (I come)	wir komm**en** (we come)
du komm**st** (you come)	ihr komm**t** (you come)
er/sie/es komm**t** (he/she/it comes)	sie/Sie komm**en** (they/you come)

singen: to sing

ich sing**e** (I sing)	wir sing**en** (we sing)
du sing**st** (you sing)	ihr sing**t** (you sing)
er/sie/es sing**t** (he/she/it sings)	sie/Sie sing**en** (they/you sing)

Sample sentences

Er kommt morgen in die Schule.
Wann kommt ihr in Berlin an?
Der Chor singt ein schönes Lied.

Stem-vowel changing verb formation

In German there are three sets of stem-vowel changing verbs: e →ie; a→ä; au→äu.

The stem-vowels changes only occur in the second and third person singular, "du" and "er/sie/es."

Stem-vowel change e →ie
sprechen: to speak

ich sprech**e** (I speak)	wir sprech**en** (we speak)
du spr**i**ch**st** (you speak)	ihr sprech**t** (you speak)
er/sie/es spr**i**ch**t** (he/she/it speaks)	sie/Sie sprech**en** (they/you speak)

Stem-vowel change a →ä
fahren: to drive

ich fahr**e** (I drive)	wir fahr**en** (we drive)
du f**ä**hr**st** (you drive)	ihr fahr**t** (you drive)
er/sie/es f**ä**hr**t** (he/she/it drives)	sie/Sie fahr**en** (they/you drive)

Stem-vowel change au →äu
laufen: to run

ich laufe (I run)	wir laufen (we run)
du läufst (you run)	ihr lauft (you run)
er/sie/es läuft (he/she/it runs)	sie/Sie laufen (they/you run)

Sample sentences

Sprecht ihr Deutsch?
Wann fährst du nach Wien?
Er läuft gern im Park.

Irregular helping verbs

German has three helping verbs: *haben, sein,* and *werden.* The formation of these three verbs is irregular and it is therefore best to memorize the conjugations of these important verbs.

haben: to have

ich habe (I have)	wir haben (we have)
du hast (you have)	ihr habt (you have)
er/sie/es hat (he/she/it has)	sie/Sie haben (they/you have)

sein: to be

ich bin (I am)	wir sind (we are)
du bist (you are)	ihr seid (you are)
er/sie/es ist (he/she/it is)	sie/Sie sind (they/you are)

werden: to become

ich werde (I become)	wir werden (we become)
du wirst (you become)	ihr werdet (you become)
er/sie/es wird (he/she/it becomes)	sie/Sie werden (they/you become)

Sample sentences

Er hat zwei Äpfel in der Hand.
Ihr seid aus Nürnberg.
Er wird Pilot.

Use of prepositions

German prepositions change the endings of the adjectives and sometimes nouns that follow them, requiring the adjectives in particular
to adopt either the accusative or dative case. Some prepositions are
strictly accusative, some are dative, and others can switch depend-
ing on how they are used. These two-way prepositions are accusative when they refer to a destination or a physical motion, and dative
when they refer to a location or an object not at motion.

Accusative prepositions

bis	until	Ich bleibe bis nächsten Sonntag./ *I am staying until next Sunday.*
durch	through	Er geht durch die Tür./ *He goes through the door.*
für	for	Ich singe ein Lied für die Mutter./ *I am singing a song for my mother.*
gegen	against	Ich bin gegen die Reformen./ *I am opposed to the reforms.*
ohne	without	Wir fahren ohne dich nach Heidelberg./ *We are going to Heidelberg without you.*
um	around	Du gehst um den Park./ *You are going around the park.*

Dative prepositions

aus	out of	Er schaut aus dem Fenster./ *He looks out of the window.*
außer	except for	Außer dir machen alle mit./ *Everyone except for you is participating.*

bei	at	Wir essen bei der Tante./ *We are eating at our aunt's house.*
mit	with	Er schreibt mit dem Bleistift./ *He writes with the pencil.*
nach	to	Nach der Arbeit gehe ich einkaufen./ *After work I go shopping.*
seit	since	Seit dem Tag wohnen wir hier./ *Since that day we live here.*
von	from	Ich habe das Auto von meinem Vater./ *I got the car from my father.*
zu	to	Ich gehe zu meiner Mutter./ *I am going to my mother.*

Two-way prepositions

an	to (accusative)	Er geht an die Tür./ *He goes to the door.*
	at (dative)	Er steht am Fenster./ *He stands at the window.*
auf	on (accusative)	Sie legt den Teller auf den Tisch./ *She puts the plate on the table.*
	on (dative)	Der Teller ist auf dem Tisch./ *The plate is on the table.*
hinter	behind (accusative)	Er geht hinter das Haus./ *He goes behind the house.*
	behind (dative)	Er steht hinter dem Haus./ *He stands behind the house.*
in	into (accusative)	Du gehst in das Haus./ *You go into the house.*
	in (dative)	Du stehst in dem Haus./ *You stand in the house.*
neben	next to (accusative)	Er legt das Buch neben das Bett./ *He puts the book next to the bed.*
	next to (dative)	Das Buch liegt neben dem Bett./ *The book lies next to the bed.*
über	over (accusative)	Er fliegt über den Atlantik./ *He flies over the Atlantic.*

	over (dative)	Er steht über dem Fluss./ *He stands over the river.*
unter	under (accusative)	Sie läuft unter den Tisch./ *She runs under the table.*
	under (dative)	Sie ist unter dem Tisch./ *She is under the table.*
vor	in front of (accusative)	Er fährt vor die Tür./ *He drives up in front of the door.*
	in front of (dative)	Er steht vor der Tür./ *He stands in front of the door.*
zwischen	between (accusative)	Das Kind geht zwischen die Autos./ *The child goes between the cars.*
	between (dative)	Das Kind steht zwischen den Autos./ *The child stands between the cars.*